WESTMAR COLL

D1034895

NEW ACCENTS
General Editor: TERENCE HAWKES

Literature and Propaganda

IN THE SAME SERIES:

Literature and Propaganda

A. P. FOULKES

METHUEN
London and New York

First published in 1983 by
Methuen & Co. Ltd
11 New Fetter Lane, London EC4P 4EE
Published in the USA by
Methuen & Co.
in association with Methuen, Inc.
733 Third Avenue, New York, NY 10017

Photoset by Rowland Phototypesetting Ltd
Bury St Edmunds, Suffolk
Printed in Great Britain by
Richard Clay (The Chaucer Press) Ltd
Bungay, Suffolk

British Library Cataloguing in Publication Data
Foulkes, A. P.
Literature and propaganda. – (New accents)
1. Propaganda
I. Title   II. Series
303.3′75   HM263

ISBN 0-416-71710-1
ISBN 0-416-71720-9 Pbk

Library of Congress Cataloging in Publication Data
Foulkes, A. Peter.
Literature and propaganda.
(New accents)
Bibliography: p.
Includes index.
1. Literature—Philosophy.
2. Propaganda.
I. Title.   II. Series: New accents (Methuen)
PN45.F58 1983   801   82-22913
ISBN 0-416-71710-1 (cased)
ISBN 0-416-71720-9 (pbk.)

Contents

General editor's preface

It is easy to see that we are living in a time of rapid and radical social change. It is much less easy to grasp the fact that such change will inevitably affect the nature of those academic disciplines that both reflect our society and help to shape it.

Yet this is nowhere more apparent than in the central field of what may, in general terms, be called literary studies. Here, among large numbers of students at all levels of education, the erosion of the assumptions and presuppositions that support the literary disciplines in their conventional form has proved fundamental. Modes and categories inherited from the past no longer seem to fit the reality experienced by a new generation.

New Accents is intended as a positive response to the initiative offered by such a situation. Each volume in the series will seek to encourage rather than resist the process of change, to stretch rather than reinforce the boundaries that currently define literature and its academic study.

Some important areas of interest immediately present themselves. In various parts of the world, new methods of analysis have been developed whose conclusions reveal the limitations of the Anglo-American outlook we inherit. New concepts of literary forms and modes have been proposed; new notions of the nature of literature itself, and of how it communicates, are current; new views of literature's role in relation to society flourish. *New Accents* will aim to expound and comment upon the most notable of these.

In the broad field of the study of human communication, more and more emphasis has been placed upon the nature and function of the new electronic media. *New Accents* will try to identify and discuss the challenge these offer to our traditional modes of critical response.

The same interest in communication suggests that the series should also concern itself with those wider anthropological and sociological areas of investigation which have begun to involve scrutiny of the nature of art itself and of its relation to our whole way of life. And this will ultimately require attention to be focused on some of those activities which in our society have hitherto been excluded from the prestigious realms of Culture. The disturbing realignment of values involved and the disconcerting nature of the pressures that work to bring it about both constitute areas that *New Accents* will seek to explore.

Finally, as its title suggests, one aspect of *New Accents* will be firmly located in contemporary approaches to language, and a continuing concern of the series will be to examine the extent to which relevant branches of linguistic studies can illuminate specific literary areas. The volumes with this particular interest will nevertheless presume no prior technical knowledge on the part of their readers, and will aim to rehearse the linguistics appropriate to the matter in hand, rather than to embark on general theoretical matters.

Each volume in the series will attempt an objective exposition of significant developments in its field up to the present as well as an account of its author's own views of the matter. Each will culminate in an informative bibliography as a guide to further study. And while each will be primarily concerned with matters relevant to its own specific interests, we can hope that a kind of conversation will be heard to develop between them: one whose accents may perhaps suggest the distinctive discourse of the future.

TERENCE HAWKES

Acknowledgements

Many friends and colleagues helped this book along in ways too numerous to list. I should like to thank especially Catherine Belsey, Karl Eckhardt, Terence Hawkes, Jens Ihwe, Peter Juhl, John Poziemski, Janice Price, Lillian Robinson, Götz Wienold and Barbara Wood.

Part of Section 9 appeared originally in *Theater und Drama in Amerika* (Edgar Lohner and Rudolf Haas (eds), 1978). I am grateful to the Erich Schmidt Verlag (Berlin) for permission to reprint it here.

The book is dedicated to Imogen and Juliet, without whom I would never have seen through *Squirrel Nutkin*.

The author and publisher would like to thank the following for kind permission to reprint copyright material: Viking Penguin Inc. and Secker & Warburg Ltd for extracts from the Introduction to Arthur Miller's *Collected Plays*, © 1957 and 1958 Arthur Miller, and extracts from Arthur Miller's *The Crucible*, © 1952 and 1953 Arthur Miller.

I

Introduction

If we refer to the nineteenth century as the Age of Ideology, then it seems even more appropriate to regard the present century as the Age of Propaganda. The radical philosophical discussion of the nineteenth century, carried on by such writers as Kant, Hegel, Schopenhauer, Comte, Spenser, Marx, Nietzsche and Mill, was essentially a western European intellectual phenomenon which only gradually and partially came to extend its influence in the form of political doctrine and social action. Twentieth-century propaganda, on the other hand, is worldwide and all-pervasive; its messages and recommended interpretations of events are not confined to a literate society, nor does it need to assume an audience which has inherited an eighteenth-century belief in progress based on mature reflection and the application of reason.

Remote communities in Africa and Latin America, although they may lack schools, medical facilities, drinking water and agricultural implements, need possess only a transistor radio in order to tune themselves in to the advertising jingles and political slogans which either desire to shape their social and economic reality or which in fact already do so. The advanced industrial societies, which to a large extent control the technology and generate the one-way communication typical of such propaganda, are themselves so saturated with propagandist practices that it has become extremely difficult to isolate and identify propaganda as a generally recognizable and describable phenomenon.

It must be admitted that most people claim the ability both to recognize and to resist propaganda, but when pressed for examples of its methods and manifestations, they usually point to the 'distortions' of the politicians they do not vote for, the 'slanted' editorials of the newspapers they tend not to read, or the 'lies' put out by the foreign power which they happen to regard as the greatest threat of the day. What they in fact recognize, according to Jacques Ellul, are the 'paper tigers', the propaganda directly opposed to their own interests whose methods 'are so absurd and obvious that even the biggest fool can manage to escape them' (Ellul 1973, p. 257). What they fail to see is that the interests they perceive as being attacked by inimical propaganda may themselves be the product of propagandistic processes far more subtle than the ones employed by the 'other side'. It is above all this invisible propaganda, which in its most successful form establishes and perpetuates itself as the common-sense of an individual or a group, which led Ellul to write of the serious 'danger of man's destruction by propaganda' (Ellul 1973, p. 257).

The relationship of literature and art to propaganda is not at all straightforward, and would in any case be dismissed as insignificant by many modern critics, whose evaluative criteria would lead them to make a distinction between 'real literature' and 'tendentious' writing. Even so, George Orwell, who stated that 'all art is to some extent propaganda' (Orwell 1970, p. 276), was probably closer to the truth than Hitler, who on one occasion was heard echoing the popular view that 'art has nothing to do with propaganda' (Balfour 1979, p. 41). Not the least of the ironies contained in these seemingly contradictory statements is the fact that Hitler's remarks were addressed to Josef Goebbels who, as head of the Reich Ministry for Popular Enlightenment and Propaganda (Reichsministerium für Volksaufklärung und Propaganda), had attempted to create a state apparatus for thought control which could have served as a model for the perfect totalitarian state depicted in Orwell's novel *Nineteen-Eighty-Four*.

Goebbels's Ministry moreover, despite Hitler's apparent claim for art's privileged status, concerned itself intensively and in intricate detail with the production and dissemination of literary works. The more spectacular moments of this activity, especially the scenes of students publicly burning the works of Heine, Thomas Mann, Brecht, etc., were recorded on newsreel and are now housed in film and TV archives around the world. That they are periodically slipped into various documentaries dealing with the Third Reich has no doubt contributed to the widespread belief that Nazi Germany is to be identified with the very essence of twentieth-century propaganda, and that by witnessing and condemning such scenes we will somehow strengthen our resistance to propagandistic messages which may be aimed directly at us by sinister forces within our own society.

Evidence for the existence of such thinking was provided a few years ago by the British Labour Party, which used some of its TV party-political broadcast time in an attempt to discredit the National Front by equating it directly, through juxtaposed images and other techniques, with National Socialism. The aim was presumably to utilize the predictable recognition of the historical enemy in order to influence the audience's attitude towards a contemporary threat. But the probable result of the campaign was that many people were made aware for the first time of the Labour Party's fear that its traditional supporters were susceptible to National Front propaganda. The Labour Party propagandists, in their attempt to illustrate the principle that those who fail to understand history will be condemned to repeat it, were no doubt also thwarted by the fact that in the popular imagination the Nazi has long ceased to be a real historical being. He now inhabits the demonic twilight of the entertainment world, the mass-produced collective subconscious within which Zulu warriors coexist with invaders from outer space and the Waffen SS. The objective correlate of such fantasy is not the National Front march with its massed Union Jacks but the apolitical motorcycle gangs wearing Nazi helmets and iron crosses.

Propaganda does not often come marching towards us waving swastikas and chanting 'Sieg Heil'; its real power lies in its capacity to conceal itself, to appear natural, to coalesce completely and indivisibly with the values and accepted power symbols of a given society. When Hitler claimed that art had nothing to do with propaganda he was anticipating a perfectly integrated National Socialist Germany whose art would spontaneously and unthinkingly reproduce the desired images and perceptions. Even in the early revolutionary period of the Third Reich, Goebbels, who had objected to the word *propaganda* being used in the title of his Ministry, insisted that 'news is best given out in such a way that it appears to be without comment but is itself tendentious' (Balfour 1979, p. 434). He was contemptuous of overtly propagandistic exercises, such as Alfred Rosenberg's *Myth of the Twentieth Century*, which he described as an 'ideological belch' (Balfour 1979, p. 43). Shortly after the Nazis assumed power he explained that there were two ways of making a revolution: 'You can go on shooting up the opposition with machine-guns until they acknowledge the superiority of the gunners. That is the simpler way. But you can also transform the nation by a mental revolution and thus win over the opposition instead of annihilating them. We National Socialists have adopted the second way and intend to pursue it' (Balfour 1979, p. 48). Goebbels's methods for pursuing these goals are worth quoting, both for the insights they provide into his view of the British press, and for the light they shed on his understanding of the relationship between propaganda and art. Claiming that propaganda was inevitable in almost any and every presentation of news, Goebbels continued:

Even the *Times*, the most democratic paper in the world, makes propaganda in that it deliberately gives prominence to certain facts, emphasizes the importance of others by writing leaders or commentaries about them, and only handles others marginally or not at all.

So I must simplify reality, omitting here, adding there. It is the same with an artist, whose picture can diverge a long way from the objective truth. What matters is that my political perception should, like the artist's aesthetic one, be genuine and true, that is to say beneficial to society. Detail doesn't matter. Truth consists in what benefits my country. (Balfour 1979, p. 431)

For Goebbels, then, the reporting of news shared with art the common feature of presenting a selective vision of 'reality' and 'objective truth'. To the extent that this selection process furthers the interests of 'society' and 'my country' it could be regarded as desirable. Since Goebbels is commonly viewed as the supreme liar of history, some readers may be uneasy in the knowledge that his definition of propaganda has lost little in topicality in the past forty years. If one were to rewrite his comments, replacing the word 'country' with such expressions as 'company', 'profit margins', 'circulation figures', 'political party', etc., the relevance of his description to contemporary advertising and electioneering becomes strikingly clear. The cliché view of the Nazi propaganda machine – lies backed up by terror – is likely to obscure rather than clarify our understanding of these similarities, and at worst will reinforce the belief that once we have seen through the paper tigers of totalitarianism we will have achieved a kind of immunity to propaganda of all kinds. Goebbels did not accomplish his ultimate aim of producing a pure National Socialist state of consciousness, and it need hardly be repeated that the Third Reich's preferred way of dealing with opposition was annihilation rather than 'mental revolution'.

On the other hand, the Nazi vocabulary and terminology which today seem so alien had by the end of the war penetrated the German language to a remarkable extent. Even the opponents of the regime, as Victor Klemperer has documented, conceptualized events and experiences in a language which had been heavily infiltrated by the philosophy of the Third Reich (Klemperer 1969, pp. 237ff.).

A similar relationship between language and ideology has been observed in comparative studies of the language of the German Democratic Republic and that of the Federal Republic of Germany. In the East German *Duden* published in 1957, for example, *fascism* is defined as a 'chauvinistic and frequently terroristic form of imperialism', whereas the West German *Duden* of 1961 glosses the word as an 'anti-democratic and nationalistic philosophy of the state' (Mueller 1973, p. 38). *Capitalism* is described in the East German version as being based on 'the exploitation of wage labour', but the West German definition emphasizes it as 'an individualistic and social order' (Mueller 1973, p. 38).

In so far as a dictionary may be part of a dominant group's attempt to control recorded knowledge and prescribe linguistic behaviour, its definitions may of course not accurately describe the actual semantic agreements which exist in a given society. Of greater interest to the analyst of propaganda is the degree to which language in its social context reflects and transmits ideology without seeming to do so. An obvious example is the way in which modern English is pervaded by the buried metaphors of capitalism: we 'exploit' opportunities, 'profit' from experiences, 'cash in' on situations once we have assessed their 'debit' and 'credit' side; we 'sell' good ideas and refuse to 'buy' the opinions of those with whom we disagree; pop-singers and politicians may become 'hot properties' once they have been taught to 'capitalize' on their talents.

If a simple principle can be derived from the discussion so far, it is that the recognition of propaganda can be seen as a function of the ideological distance which separates the observer from the act of communication observed. This principle cannot be made to yield a formal definition of propaganda, for it is in the first place a statement about the subjectivity of perception and the relationship of perception to the values, beliefs and assumptions of the group or community with which the individual identifies. The principle does possess a certain explanatory usefulness, however, for it permits us to examine more closely the divergent points of view for which Orwell and Hitler were taken earlier as examples. Hitler's assertion that art has nothing to do with propaganda does not contradict Orwell's statement that all art is propaganda, but is rather contained within it, for the propaganda-free art which Hitler envisaged was an art within which the values and beliefs of National Socialism would be dominant, invisible and totally natural. This 'illusion of pure aestheticism' was for Orwell a reminder that 'propaganda in some form or other lurks in every book, that every work of art has a meaning and a purpose – a political, social and religious purpose – that our aesthetic judgements are always coloured by our prejudices and beliefs' (Orwell 1970, p. 152).

Hitler's words, moreover, reveal a dilemma that confronts all totalitarian regimes which attempt to use art as a vehicle for propaganda, namely that art and literature are capable of producing a counter-vision which in turn creates the sense of ideological distance which renders propaganda visible. In the occupied Polish territories the Nazis acted on this knowledge with an unparalleled ruthlessness: libraries were closed; dictionaries, atlases and the Polish classics were confiscated; special writing teams were established to produce a steady stream of soft pornography and sensationalism; even the possession of a radio became a capital offence (Brenner 1963, p. 138). In Germany itself, such harshness was precluded by the fact that the Nazis wanted to appropriate the German classics for their own purposes, and thus in 1934 books appeared with such titles as *Schiller as Hitler's Comrade-in-Arms: National Socialism in Schiller's Dramas* (by Hans Fabricius).

These attempts to Nazify the past were not totally successful, for in 1941 a directive issued by the Reich Chancellery banned performances of Schiller's *William Tell* and withdrew the play as a school text (Taylor 1980, pp. 240–1; Brenner 1963, p. 209). Despite such vigilance, and notwithstanding the censorship and suppression of authors, texts and even literary commentary (Strothmann 1963, p. 283), Hitler's controllers of culture were constantly reminded of art's disconcerting potential for subversion. Even the popular light entertainment meted out to the troops in the later years of the war proved itself capable of appropriation in a manner far more effective than the official attempts to make Nazis out of Goethe and Schiller. British observers of German public opinion and morale, for example, were quick to note the significance of the growing popularity of a song containing the words:

> Es geht alles vorüber,
> Es geht alles vorbei.
> Nach jedem Dezember
> Kommt wieder ein Mai.

(It all passes over/It all drifts away./Every December/Leads on to a May.) The Wehrmacht, adding its own tribute to the many which National Socialism had unwittingly paid to the power of literature, banned the song before the end of the war on account of its 'fatalist' message (Balfour 1979, p. 324).

2

What is propaganda?

An inquiry into the mode of existence of propaganda has two aspects, both of which are related to central questions concerning the nature of literature. In the first place we can ask about the cultural, social and historical conditions within which propaganda is produced: When and why does it appear? Whose interests does it serve? How is it 'consumed', and by whom? But we could also investigate the formal aspects of propaganda, attempting to describe the way it functions as a system, or as a set of systems, and seeking to differentiate it from other forms of communication. The same questions are asked of course about literature, and although they have not been answered to everyone's theoretical satisfaction, the very asking of them is facilitated by a general social agreement that a certain body of texts, and the writing and reading of them, constitute the phenomenon of 'literature'. Propaganda, as we have seen, is a far more elusive concept to define, partly because its recognition or supposed recognition is often a function of the relative historical viewpoint of the person observing it.

Because of this elusiveness, many investigators of propaganda have limited themselves to extreme situations, such as war, where it is comparatively easy to identify communication intended to demoralize the enemy or strengthen the resolve of one's own side. Michael Balfour's *Propaganda in War 1939–1945* is more illuminating than many such studies, mainly because its account of the organizations and policies of war-time propaganda differentiates carefully between the way in which information was structured for home consumption and the way it was transmitted to the enemy, both by the British and the Germans.

Balfour distinguishes five categories of propaganda: false statements made in the genuine belief that they are true; deliberate lies; *suggestio falsi* (i.e. the suggestion of falsehood, for example the information leaks and military activity designed to suggest to the Germans that the Allied landing would not take place in Normandy); *suppressio veri* (i.e. the suppression of truth – an example is the way in which the British Government concealed the extent of damage caused by German flying bombs in the Second World War. Goebbels's own propaganda, which desperately needed facts about the destruction caused by the 'wonder weapons', was frustrated by this silence. On the other hand, ploys of this kind can rebound on the propagandist if the domestic population, which may have access to the truth, interprets the suppression of information as an attempt to conceal casualty figures from the public); the slanting of news (Balfour 1979, pp. 427–32). All five involve the active participation of a propagandist, for even the first category implies the conscious fabrication of falsehood, usually with the intent to have it transmitted unsuspectingly through a respected or authoritative channel. The 'propagandist' is not to be identified on all occasions with the 'author', however, for, as Richard Taylor points out in his study of Soviet and Nazi film propaganda, one of the functions of the propagandist is to create new contexts of meaning for familiar messages by 'activating propaganda potential' (Taylor 1979, p. 21). During the First World War, for example, the British Army put out a series of broadsheets, conveniently just the right size to be slipped into an envelope being sent to the Front, containing various patriotic poems and prose pieces. Some of the material was written on demand, but much of it was taken directly from Wordsworth, Shakespeare and so on (Taylor 1979, pp. 20–1). The defining characteristic of propaganda for Taylor is in fact the existence of the propagandist; if we cannot establish a link between the propagandist and his or her audience, then we cannot speak of 'propaganda' (Taylor 1979, p. 21).

This insistence on the identifiable presence of a propagandist can be misleading when it confirms the common notion of propaganda as 'the work of a few evil men, seducers of the people, cheats and authoritarian rulers who want to dominate a population' (Ellul 1973, p. 118). This view, Jacques Ellul continues,

> always thinks of propaganda as being made voluntarily; it assumes that a man decides 'to make propaganda', that a government establishes a Propaganda Ministry, and that things just develop from there on. According to this view, the public is just an object, a passive crowd that one can manipulate, influence, and use. (Ellul 1973, p. 118)

This popular view of propaganda is not the only one rejected decisively in Ellul's comprehensive and pioneering *Propaganda: The Formation of Men's Attitudes*. He sees the tendency to equate propaganda with 'lies' as likely to further the interests of propaganda by concealing its nature as 'an enterprise for perverting the significance of events' behind a façade of un-assailable 'factuality' (Ellul 1973, p. 58). It is in this sense that education, despite its professed belief in the liberating effect of literacy, can be seen as a pre-propagandist process through which facts are interpreted according to the symbols which express a group's collective ideas about its past and its future (Ellul 1973, pp. 108–12). Ellul's account is disturbingly pro-vocative, even though he occasionally slips into a mood of what has been rightly criticized as 'Aristotelian Christian pessimism' (Szanto 1978, p. 205). I shall return later to some of his arguments and examples, but would first like to summarize a section of his book in which he makes a crucial distinction between two types of propaganda, the understanding of which is essential to a discussion of propaganda in literature.

In his attempt to define categories of propaganda, Ellul (1973, pp. 61–87) makes four distinctions within the general phenomenon. Each of these distinctions embraces a pair of types, the first one of which is associated with popular views of 'classic' propaganda. The four distinctions he makes are be-tween: 1 political and sociological propaganda; 2 agitation and integration; 3 vertical and horizontal propaganda; 4 rational and irrational propaganda.

Political propaganda appears when a group, usually a government or one of its agencies, uses techniques of influence in order to achieve goals which are clearly distinguished and quite precise. *Sociological* propaganda, on the other hand, is a sort of 'persuasion from within' (Ellul 1973, p. 64), which results when an individual has accepted or assimilated the dominant economic and political ideologies of his society and uses them as a basis for making what he regards as spontaneous choices and value judgements. The two types are not of course necessarily contradictory in aim or effect, for the American Way of Life could be presented as a series of desirable goals by a CIA-financed radio station just as it could emerge naturally from the pages of *Reader's Digest*.

The propaganda of *agitation* is usually subversive and oppositional. It may seek to overthrow a government or established order, but may equally be used by governments, for example in times of war, when they wish to break down the 'psychological barriers of habit, belief, and judgment' (Ellul 1973, p. 72). It can be understood as a call for action, whereas the propaganda of *integration*, as a long-term, 'self-reproducing propaganda that seeks to obtain stable behaviour in terms of the permanent social setting' (Ellul 1973, p. 75), is more properly regarded as a process designed to produce inertia, or at least conformity. Both agitation and integration propaganda can be *vertical*, in the sense that they can emanate from a leader seeking to influence the masses, or they can be *horizontal*, i.e. made 'inside the group (not from the top), where, in principle, all individuals are equal and there is no leader' (Ellul 1973, p. 81). The distinction between *rational* and *irrational* propaganda, finally, is drawn in order to dispel the common belief that there exists an essential difference between 'factual information' aimed at the intellect, and propaganda addressed always to feelings and passion. Just as there is rational advertising, based on technical descriptions and empirical data, there is also rational propaganda based exclusively on 'facts, statistics, economic ideas' (Ellul 1973, p. 84). Propaganda can thus be 'honest, strict, exact, but its effect remains irrational because of the spontaneous transformation of all its contents by the individual' (Ellul 1973, p. 87). In other words, the rational can be made to function irrationally. This last point was anticipated in Orwell's dictum that 'All propaganda is lies, even when one is telling the truth' (Orwell 1970, p.465).

Ellul's categories should not be regarded as water-tight definitions, but rather as attempts to capture for descriptive purposes the significant moments of a complex process. It should also be noted that they can overlap and intersect in various ways, some of them quite bewildering. When Hitler purged the SA in 1934, for example, he backed up his action with a campaign of agitation propaganda which was vertical and irrational. The purge itself, however, can be seen historically as marking the growing Nazi awareness that their long-term goals would best be served through a process of integration. Just sixteen days after the blood-letting Hitler was claiming in a speech that 'Revolution is not a permanent process . . . . The ideas in our programme impose an obligation upon us not to act like fools and to overthrow everything, but to actualize our thinking cleverly and carefully' (Craig 1978, p. 587). As Germany came closer to war, what in fact developed was a situation in which the Germans were subjected simultaneously to agitation and integration propaganda. Even Goebbels, who among the Nazi leaders was the most convinced of the power of a rational and horizontal integration propaganda, demonstrated a spectacular mastery of vertical agitation propaganda in his 'Do you want total war' speech delivered at the Berlin Sports Palace in 1943 (Moltmann 1964, pp. 13—43).

The distinction made by Ellul between agitation and integration is essential to a discussion of propaganda in literature. Before this point can be developed more fully, we will have to investigate the nature of literature as a process with a view to identifying those areas where it can coincide with various propagandistic processes, but even a quick anticipatory glance will illustrate the explanatory usefulness of the distinction.

Traditionally, for example, it has been customary to divide literature into 'good' works and 'bad' works. The aesthetic criteria on which such judgements are based are not clearly established, and indeed the history of literature is littered with arguments concerning the relative 'greatness' or otherwise of individual authors and texts. Within Ellul's distinction one could differentiate works which question and subvert value systems and beliefs from works which assimilate and reinforce such systems, and one could *then* proceed to an inquiry into the values which inform the reading and critical reception of the works. Extreme instances of such processes can be observed in the literature surrounding revolution and radical social change, for, as Ellul points out, 'once the revolutionary party has taken power, it must begin immediately to operate with integration propaganda' (Ellul 1973, p. 76), which usually means that 'other propagandists must be employed, as totally different qualities are required for integration propaganda' (Ellul 1973, p. 77). This of course is the process parodied in Orwell's *Animal Farm*, which describes how the stirring song 'Beasts of England' is banned in favour of the ode to 'Comrade Napoleon' which contains the lines 'Every beast great or small/Sleeps at peace in his stall' (Orwell 1980, pp. 47–8).

With regard to the Soviet Union, this type of post-revolutionary development, often referred to dismissively by Western critics as 'Zhdanovism', has been described as

> a self-mutilating process whereby a post-revolutionary society cuts away the ideas and the ideology which had created that very society; a process whereby Marxism and early Soviet Communism (Bolshevism) were converted into a conformist dogma based largely on the pre-Marxist and pre-Leninist Russian populist-democratic intellectual heritage. (Solomon 1979, p. 292)

Soviet aesthetics as promulgated by Andrei Zhdanov certainly provide numerous examples of regressive thinking. The very terms of opprobrium used (decadence, baseness, primitive, dung-heap, depravity, corruption, vulgarity, etc.) evoke the repressed sexuality of Victorian times rather than the sexual liberation championed by many of the early revolutionaries (Solomon 1979, p. 240). Of greater significance, however, are the tendencies and attitudes towards art which Solomon indicates as being typical of all post-revolutionary periods – rejection of complexity, the desire to create exemplary myths, censorship and, above all, an awareness of and hence a fear of art's capacity to subvert. Jürgen Rühle, in his detailed *Literature and Revolution: A Critical Study of the Writer and Communism in the Twentieth Century*, provides some fascinating insights into the nature of literary commitment both before and after the revolution. Despite a certain evangelical stridency, which at times borders on cold-war rhetoric, Rühle's chronicle offers a wealth of information which can be seen to illustrate Ellul's categories of agitation and integration. Vladimir Mayakovsky, for example, who once stated 'I want/ . . . the pen to be on a par/with the bayonet' (Rühle 1969, p. 15), was rightly considered to be one of the brilliant literary agitators of the revolution, but he slowly grew to understand that the post-revolutionary demands for integration, which denounced Trotsky's belief in permanent revolution as a heresy, had little use for his talents. By 1929, the year before he took his own life, he was using his verse to deride:

> Lickspittles . . .
> sectarians
>   and bibbers. –
> Chest thrown out
> they stalk along
>   proudly,
> all decked with badges
>   and fountain pens (Rühle 1969, p. 17)

The literary history of East Germany is in some respects a repeat performance of what happened in the Soviet Union. The reputations of various authors have waxed and waned against a background of brief 'thaws' interpunctuated by government-launched campaigns against 'formalism' and 'modernism'. Some writers, notably Anna Seghers and Johannes Becher, were able to accommodate their talents to the demands of a regime which now wished to consolidate its power rather than agitate for it, but others such as Bertolt Brecht and Friedrich Wolf, both of whom had earned their laurels as literary agitators in the 1920s, found it more difficult to function as legitimators of the status quo. The official East German history of the state's literature, without providing any real details, explains that Brecht and Wolf, whose task after the war was to 'portray a society in the transition to socialism and a humanity now freed from exploitation' (Haase *et al.* 1976, p. 352), experienced difficulties 'springing from the hitherto unknown reality' of the object to be depicted. 'Apart from Soviet drama, there were no experiences of this situation', and both authors died too soon to 'acquire such knowledge and explore the unaccustomed'

(Haase *et al.* 1976, p. 352). In fact both Brecht and Wolf – and scores of writers in the GDR (German Democratic Republic) in the past twenty years – were induced by their very knowledge of Soviet literature to struggle for a committed art which retained the right to question official truth.

It is true that Brecht, although distressed by the hostility and misunderstanding which greeted some of his productions in East Berlin (documented by Rühle 1969, pp. 235ff.), was prepared to co-operate with the authorities in what he perceived to be an uneven but progressive advance towards communism. An incident in 1953, however, reveals strikingly the contempt which Brecht the agitator felt for the writers who had become propagandists of integration. Following the strikes and disturbances in East Berlin on 17 June, Kuba (the pen-name of Kurt Barthel, Secretary of the GDR Writer's Union) had quickly put together a pamphlet which was distributed among striking workers in the Stalin-Allee. Headed 'How I am ashamed', Kuba's paternalistic message was addressed to 'Bricklayers, Painters, Carpenters', and went on to explain how well the workers had been fed by the state, and how inspiring it was to know that the people's police had refrained from firing on the insurgent crowds. 'You can now go to bed like good children at nine o'clock,' Kuba continued, 'the Soviet Army and the comrades of the German people's police will watch over you and over the peace of the world. . . . It is easy to repair destroyed houses, but very very difficult to rebuild destroyed confidence (in you)' (Wagenbach, Stephan and Krüger, pp. 119–120). Brecht described the distribution of the leaflet in a poem, published after his death, which concluded scathingly: 'Would it not/then be easier for the government/to dissolve the people/ and elect a new one?' (Wagenbach, Stephan and Krüger, pp. 119–20).

Currently, the cultural policies of the GDR are still beset by the problem of agitation vis-à-vis integration, but an interesting recent development is that the authorities in the East seem to want to export their agitators and dissidents to West Germany, where they can presumably do more harm (or good), rather than incur international displeasure by imprisoning them or censoring their writings. A case in point is Wolf Biermann, a native of Hamburg whose Marxist convictions led him to move to East Berlin in 1953, and who in the late 1950s and early 1960s became internationally known as the composer and performer of political lyrics reminiscent of Villon and the early Brecht. Biermann was made welcome as long as he sang of imperialist aggression, and was tolerated even when he began to criticize some aspects of GDR society. But he swiftly fell into disfavour when he echoed the 'melancholy vision of deep conflicts whipped up by western controllers of opinion' in songs which questioned and satirized the 'anti-fascist protective barrier' (Haase *et al.* 1976, p. 491), i.e. the Berlin Wall.

The Central Committee of the SED (Socialist Unity Party) used the occasion of its eleventh plenary meeting in 1965 to mount a campaign against 'modernist', 'scepticist', 'anarchistic', 'nihilistic', 'liberalist' and 'pornographic' tendencies in contemporary literature (Emmerich 1981, p. 130). Biermann, who had been banned from performing in 1964, was singled out for special condemnation on account of his 'ill-disguised bourgeois-anarchistic socialism' and 'strongly pornographic traits' (Emmerich 1981, p. 130). In November 1976, when Biermann was performing in West Germany at the invitation of a trade-union group, he was deprived of his citizenship by the East German government and thus prevented from returning to the GDR. The SED newspaper *Neues Deutschland* attempted to justify this step by declaring that 'citizenship implied a sense of loyalty towards the state' (Emmerich 1981, p. 188), but this and other official explanations did not deter scores of well-known GDR writers from making a public protest against the expulsion. The government responded with a wave of new restrictive measures, ranging from imprisonment and house-arrest to censorship and party disciplinary proceedings. Currency exchange regulations were invoked to penalize authors receiving royalties from West Germany, and in 1979 the criminal code was revised so as to permit prison sentences of up to eight years for authors passing on to foreign organizations or individuals manuscripts 'likely to harm the interests of the German Democratic Republic' (Emmerich 1981, p. 192).

This latter measure, which served to intensify the uneasy situation of East German writers by making them responsible for meanings which might be attached to their works in the West, was calculated to strengthen the propaganda of integration by inducing a state of self-censorship, which is ultimately far more effective than direct intervention by government censors. At the same time, the protests precipitated by the Biermann affair seem to have permitted GDR cultural functionaries to identify writers and intellectuals deemed incapable of integration, for in the late 1970s an unprecedented number of visas was issued to authors wanting to move to West Germany. This again was a cynical step, for although the official interpreters of GDR literature had attacked Biermann for writing poems which 'function in the Federal Republic and West Berlin as an instrument of imperialist policy inimical to the GDR' (Haase *et al.* 1976, p. 491), they no doubt derived some satisfaction from the fact that Biermann, a few months after his arrival in the West, was writing songs describing the transition as a move 'from the frying pan into the mire' ('Vom Regen in die Jauche', literally, 'from the rain into the piss', a word-play on the proverb 'Vom Regen in die Traufe', 'from the rain into the gutter').

The existence of the two Germanies with their competing ideological apparatuses provides endless opportunities for observing modern propaganda as an 'enterprise for perverting the significance of events' (Ellul 1973, p. 58). This does not mean that events possess a pure and absolute significance which can be tampered with, but rather that the schemes of interpretation which prevail at a given time, even though they appear to be natural and spontaneous, may derive from the various processes defined by Ellul as propaganda. Bearing Ellul's categories in mind, we will now look more closely at the phenomenon of literature and the schemes of interpretation which have collected themselves around it.

3
The process of literary communication

Just as it would be an oversimplification to identify propaganda arbitrarily as a particular group of texts, or as specific instances of intended manipulation, or as the effect of certain messages on someone's actions, it is equally misleading to define 'literature' solely in terms of one of its many aspects. Although there is general agreement that a certain body of texts constitutes 'literature', literary theories from Aristotle to the present have recognized that the term refers not only to texts, but also to a network of relationships which involve the text in a series of causes, intentions, effects and acts of mediation. In the twentieth century, however, as literature gained an independent position of respect in the educational curricula of many societies, numerous attempts were made to define the proper object of literary study and to specify the nature of the acts of mediation pertinent to it. Around the middle of the century the discussion was dominated by concepts of the 'concrete, literary work of art', and criticism which attached importance to the relationship obtaining between the text and authorial intention, or the text and reader response, was frequently dismissed as being outside the true scope of literary studies; they were examples of 'extrinsic' methods, which may be relevant to such disciplines as psychology and sociology, but which must be prevented from displacing the 'intrinsic' criticism necessary to the understanding of literature as a discrete phenomenon (cf. Wellek and Warren 1956).

The shifting perspectives and suppositions of modern criticism have been well documented by many scholars, some of
whom have drawn attention to the ideological implications of
methods which seek to determine the way in which we understand literary works. Eagleton sees both literature and criticism
as caught up in a 'spiral of mutual reinforcements' in which the
'literary text naturalizes experience' while criticism 'naturalizes
the text. Under the form of an illumination, criticism renders
natural the text's necessary self-blindness' (Eagleton 1976, p.
18). Fredric Jameson has argued persuasively for the 'priority of
the political interpretation of literary texts' and for 'the political
perspective not as some supplementary method . . . but rather
as the absolute horizon of all reading and interpretation' (Jameson 1981, p. 17). Jameson rejects the 'convenient working
distinction between cultural texts that are social and political
and those that are not'; such a distinction 'becomes worse than
an error: namely, a symptom and a reinforcement of the reifica-
tion and privatization of contemporary life' (Jameson 1981, p.
20). Catherine Belsey, whose recently published *Critical Practice*
owes much to the influential literary discussion conducted in
France over the past twenty years, surveys the main trends of
post-romantic criticism against her aim of redrawing the 'map
of "Eng. Lit."' (Belsey 1980, p.109), of producing a critical
practice which would recognize the way in which meanings
'circulate between text, ideology and readers whose subjectivity
is discursively constructed and so displayed across a range of
discourses' (Belsey 1980, p. 140). Although Belsey rejects critical methods which view the author as a determinant of meaning,
arguing that once the text is 'released from the constraints of a
single and univocal reading' it 'becomes available for production, plural, contradictory, capable of change' (Belsey 1980, p.
134), she is more circumspect in her definition of production
than Tony Bennett, for whom the task of criticism is 'that of
actively politicizing the text, of *making its politics for it*, by producing
a new position for it within the field of cultural relations and,
thereby, new forms of use and effectivity within the broader
social process' (Bennett 1979, p. 168).

Bennet's concept of a liberated but politicized criticism,
based on the premise that 'the text is not the issuing source of
meaning' (Bennett 1979, p. 174), reveals clearly the capacity of

literary criticism to become a process for controlling the way in which meanings are attached to signs. In one way, his advocacy of a criticism which has unmoored itself from both the author and the text can be viewed as part of a larger trend which has championed the reader's right to understand literature in whatsoever manner he or she chooses. But since the purpose of this freedom is that of 'actively politicizing' the text, Bennett has not really moved outside the company of those who wish to influence the processes of construing literary meaning. From the viewpoint of text-related interpretation his study has been described as 'sinister', and 'no more bothered with the niceties of what books actually say than was the old Marxist critic-in-chief, Andrey Zhdanov' (Bellos 1980, p. 122).

But what do books 'actually say'? Or more precisely, how are literary texts perceived to possess meaning, and under what conditions do we attach meanings to them? In so far as a novel or a poem can be translated into another language, we may be justified in claiming that it possesses 'empirical meaning', defined by Quine as 'what the sentences of one language and their firm translation in a completely alien language have in common' (Quine 1964, p. 460). But as every literary translator knows, even this empirical meaning is likely to be distorted as it moves from one semantic system and cultural context into another. A well-known example is afforded by the first sentence of Franz Kafka's novel *The Trial*, which states that Joseph K. was 'arrested one fine morning'. In English the verb 'to arrest' can mean to stop a process as well as to take into custody, and a well-known American interpretation of the novel is based on this double meaning (Fromm 1951). Since the German verb used by Kafka, 'verhaften', does not permit this particular dual meaning, critics have accused Fromm of violating the semantic integrity of the original, of ignoring what the book 'actually says'. Yet suppose that the verb 'verhaften' were to extend its field of meaning over the next hundred years or so and acquire the possibility of describing the stopping of a process. Would critics then be justified in interpreting *The Trial* as Fromm does?

When the question has been posed in these terms we can readily see that the problem of empirical meaning embraces works in our own language from which we may be separated culturally and semantically, as well as foreign texts. But this fact, far from resolving the difficulty, leads us straight to another of the many controversies of modern criticism. The student of Shakespeare, for example, might be urged by one mentor to familiarize himself thoroughly with Elizabethan history, language and culture as an essential first step towards a 'proper understanding'. In the very act of doing so, however, the student might run across passages telling him that 'it can never be an argument against the interpretation of this or that passage in Shakespeare that a usage is presupposed which did not exist in the English of Shakespeare's time' (Bateson 1968, p. 6).

From my own experience I know that many British and American critics, explicitly or implicitly associating the study of literature with notions of political freedom, profess to see a healthy 'pluralism' in the existence of competing methodologies and critical practices. Yet such a view is naive when it ignores the fact that many of today's rival hypotheses imply the total denial of other metacritical positions. Even if we begin with the assumption that literature is a communicative process, involving an author, a text and readers (and many theorists would reject such an assumption), we encounter intense disagreement concerning the proper method of defining aspects of the process. We find real authors and implied authors, texts and metatexts, empirical readers, 'competent speaker' readers, super-readers and, more recently, implied readers. The object of study may again be the unconscious of the author (real or implied), while the text, too, is held by some to possess its own unconscious, the identification of which allows us to understand what the text cannot say, which in the case of some texts is considered to be more significant than what it does say. The text may be regarded as a structure of authorially willed meaning, or it may be a kind of public oracle, and as such it may or may not require the mediating services of initiates. Some texts are supposed to refer to the real world; all texts, runs the counter-argument, refer to a fictive world. A third view is that texts, because they consist of language, and because language merely seems to impose order on a continuum, can refer only to what we perceive to be the real world.

For the purposes of describing literary propaganda, it is fortunately not necessary to enter this highly charged arena in order to assess the different methods either in their own terms or in those of the opposition. But since criticism can function as a process which controls the perception of another process – in this case literature – and can thus itself operate as propaganda, we do need a position 'outside' criticism which will permit us to see in a general way how the two processes are related to each other. The basis for such a position can be found in the semiotic theories of Charles Morris, especially in his treatment of the concept of meaning.

Morris describes the sign process, which he terms semiosis, as a three-dimensional phenomenon consisting of semantics, syntactics and pragmatics. Semantics studies the relationship which obtains between signs and designata (when these are existent entities, they are called denotata); syntactics examines the relations between signs and other signs, while pragmatics concerns itself with the relationship between signs and their interpreters (who in the case of literature would comprise both authors and readers).

The word 'meaning' can obscure rather than clarify our understanding for all too often it is used without prior definition to refer to separate aspects of the sign process, for example to designata or denotata, to the total process of semiosis, or to pragmatic aspects such as notions of significance or value (Morris 1971, p. 55). Morris takes up this problem with reference to art in his important essay *Esthetics and the Theory of Signs* (first published in 1939). Although the essay is impregnated with formalistic aesthetic views which Morris had borrowed from contemporaries (Foulkes 1975, pp. 34ff.), it none the less indicates a framework within which the 'devotees of the various "isms"' might be located in the 'dark jungle of esthetic criticism' (Morris 1971, p. 432). Briefly, Morris accuses different schools of criticism of distortion when they emphasize one aspect of semiosis at the expense of the other two, and when in consequence 'various descriptions of aspects of a complex process are taken to be rival accounts of the whole process' (Morris 1971, p. 430). Moreover, an act of criticism may even completely confuse one dimension of the sign process with another; a pragmatic analysis, for example, might believe itself to be a semantic analysis, or might even masquerade as a semantic analysis in order to win the approval of a particular school of criticism.

In order to develop these points more fully, we need to borrow one further concept from Morris, that of the *interpretant*. Within Morris's system the *interpreter* is 'any organism for which something is a sign', while the *interpretant* is 'the disposition to respond, because of the sign, by response sequences of some behavior-family' (Morris 1971, p. 93). And again, the interpretant is 'a disposition to respond in certain ways under certain circumstances' (Morris 1971, p. 105). Morris provides his most succinct description of the sign process in the first chapter of *Signification and Significance*, where he explains it as a five-term relation – v, w, x, y, z, – 'in which v sets up in w the disposition to react in a certain kind of way, x, to a certain kind of object, y (not then acting as a stimulus), under certain conditions, z' (Morris 1971, pp. 401–2). In cases where such a relation obtains, v would be the sign, w the interpreter of the sign, x the interpretant (disposition to interpret in a certain way), y the signification and z the context in which the sign occurs. Morris illustrates the process by means of an interesting example derived from Frisch's investigations into the communication system of bees:

> Karl von Frisch has shown that a bee which finds nectar is able, on returning to the hive, to 'dance' in such a way as to direct other bees to the food source. In this case the dance is the sign; the other bees affected by the dance are interpreters; the disposition to react in a certain kind of way by these bees, because of the dance, is the interpretant; the kind of object toward which the bees are prepared to act in this way is the signification of the sign; and the position of the hive is part of the context. (Morris 1971, p. 402)

As an aspect of human communication, the interpretant would not normally lead to an automatic conditioned response, for the individual's ability to produce 'personal post-language symbols' (i.e. to think) permits him to 'signify to himself the consequences' of behaviour (Morris 1971, p. 278). One can signify, for example, 'the reliability, or adequacy, of certain signs or the purpose for which someone else is producing a given sign', and therefore 'the effect of a given sign on behavior may be dependent in subtle and complex ways upon the signs which intervene before the incidence of the sign in question, or before the stimulus for which it is preparatory' (Morris 1971, p. 278). In a note to this section Morris suggests that hypnosis and certain forms of propaganda 'seem to cut down the intervening sign-processes of which the individual is capable, and thus allow the interpretants of the signs with which the individual is confronted to take overt form more directly and quickly – laughing when something is signified as funny, crying when something is signified as unfortunate, responding to commands in an almost automatic fashion' (Morris 1971, p. 296).

Examples of interpretants being manipulated in order to elicit a desired response to sign sequences can readily be identified in the media, and in the communicative systems of politics and advertising. A crude but obvious instance is the TV laughing machine, an apparatus designed to put social pressure on the individual viewer to conform to group behaviour, even though the behaviour may be nothing more than the artificially mechanized wish of a scriptwriter or sponsor. Similarly, tele-vised political speeches may be staged in such a way that the camera takes in nods of assent and approval from figures of respect. In societies with a strong patriotic tradition, the nation-al flag may serve as a stage prop in order to dispose the audience to believe in the speaker's commitment to the interests of the country as a whole. In this case, an established sign functions as an interpretant for other signs (the political speech). In most cases, however, the interpretant, as a 'disposition to respond in certain ways under certain circumstances', derives not from the immediate context of a sign but from the process of socialization and integration to which the individual is subjected by his or her society. An extreme illustration of how rules of interpretation are internalized is to be found in Aldous Huxley's *Brave New World*, where children in the Infant Nurseries are conditioned through alarm bells and electric shocks to develop what they will later come to regard as an instinctive hatred of books.

In his own analysis of different types of discourse, Morris defines propagandistic discourse, which he admits is 'somewhat difficult to isolate', as prescriptive/systemic. Prescriptors are 'signs which signify to their interpreters the required perform-ance of a specific response to some object or situation' (Morris 1971, p. 161), while in the systemic use of signs 'the aim is simply to organize sign-produced behavior, that is, to organize the interpretants of other signs' (Morris 1971, p. 183). Morris's account of one of the ways in which this process works is worth quoting at length, for it illustrates how vertical political propaganda can insinuate itself into language and thus become self-perpetuating integration:

> The speaker changes the denotation of certain common terms while continuing to use the existing appraisive and prescriptive features of their signification. The defender of the status quo will call anyone a 'Communist' who proposes social changes as long as the term carries the power of prescribing repressive measures to anyone so denoted. Or a term like 'free' will, in certain democratic societies, be extended to any existing practices that a person wishes to perpetuate – since in such societies the protection and extension of freedom is prescribed morally and approved politically. Such a use of terms is really a prescriptive metaphor since it extends the denotation of signs in terms of a similarity of prescriptions with respect to the old and the new denotata. (Morris 1971, p. 226)

Morris's description of aesthetic communication as a sign process, together with his concept of the interpretant, permit some interesting observations on the nature of literature and propaganda. If the language of a literary text, as Richard Kuhns has suggested, is 'already an interpretation of realities we must discover' (Kuhns 1972, p. 105), then an understanding of the forces which may attempt to control our discovery of those realities is as important to our understanding of the text as is the relationship of the text to the realities it purports to convey. In other words, both the text and those acts which mediate it can function systemically in order to organize the interpretants of other signs.

A simple example of both processes at work can be seen in Maurice Bowra's discussion of Tennyson's poem 'The Charge of the Light Brigade'. The poem itself functions as an interpretant by positioning an image of thrilling heroism between the British public and a reality of carnage and official ineptitude. For various reasons the modern reader would tend to reject such an interpretant, and Bowra seems to concede this point in his commentary: 'When he (Tennyson) tactfully reduced the cause of this insane exploit to the words "Someone had blunder'd", he might in our judgement have shirked the most troubling feature of the whole affair.' But having granted this, Bowra then goes on to reconstruct the historical context of the poem, within which Tennyson 'would certainly reflect public opinion that this was no time to distribute open blame, since it might detract from the magnificence of the charge . . . . At a time when the British people sorely needed to feel that its achievements in the recent battle were worthy of its military past, Tennyson gave it what it wanted' (Bowra 1966, pp. 4–5).

The point at issue here is not that Bowra makes Tennyson sound like Goebbels after Stalingrad, but rather that the particular application of an historical method suggests subtly that a modern understanding of the poem would be inappropriate, incomplete. The act of understanding is reduced to an observation of how others supposedly understood. In the terms of Morris's semiotic categories, the elucidation of a pragmatic relationship (between the poem and its contemporary readers) is beginning to emerge as 'meaning'. When Bowra later discusses the anti-Nazi songs which Brecht composed in the 1930s, one might be justified in expecting a similar emphasis on pragmatic historical relationships, but this time the aesthetic dimension is held to be the important one: 'In all this there is undoubted power, but we miss the fullness of Brecht's daemonic impact. He has curbed his genius in order to drive his message home, and his message is poorer in consequence' (Bowra 1966, p. 122).

Properly speaking, Bowra is still discussing a pragmatic relationship for his words presuppose readers who can judge such things as 'fullness', 'daemonic impact' and 'genius'. Once we have accepted these readers as our guides, we begin to see how Brecht's message becomes 'poorer', while by accepting the views attributed to Tennyson's contemporaries we may understand the 'desperate thrill and the unquestioned heroism of the exploit', and the 'astonishing revelation of discipline and self-sacrifice' (Bowra 1966, pp. 4–5).

All this should not be taken to suggest that Bowra sets out deliberately to manipulate his reader's understanding of various literary works. On the contrary, when *Poetry and Politics* appeared in 1966 it was a timely reminder to many British and

American critics that literature had through the centuries concerned itself with public events, and even though Bowra addresses himself primarily to 'authentic poetry which defies the corrosion of time' (Bowra 1966, p. 1), he illuminates strikingly the process whereby the poetry of public patriotism – 'phantoms of martial grandeur and belligerent virility' – receded in the face of a more vital private vision of 'harsh realities' portrayed by 'relentlessly truthful witnesses' (Bowra 1966, p. 13).

What is significant is that even within this framework of open-minded liberal rationality we can find examples of interpretants being organized in such a way that they constrain understanding. Morris's semiotic categories can provide some formal explanation of how this happens, but in order to speculate on why it should happen we need to locate this type of criticism within a broader cultural and historical context. Claus Mueller, in his study of the political sociology of language, provides an analysis of advanced industrial society which sees the liberal middle class, traditionally the group whose loyalty to the established order was beyond question, as being caught up in a 'process of delegitimation' (Mueller 1973, p. 10). His thesis implies an ambivalence in the contemporary liberal mentality which on the one hand is alienated from the successful integrating ideologies of the past but which on the other still controls 'secondary socialization agencies, such as educational and informational institutions'. To the extent that these agencies 'reinforce deprivation by propagating rationalizations or by avoiding pertinent discussion' (Mueller 1973, p. 23) they may prevent other groups from articulating or indeed from even perceiving 'the structural source of deprivation' (Mueller 1973, p. 162).

Although Mueller does not make the point explicitly, it seems to me that his analysis sheds light on the peculiar mixture of illumination and mystification which pervades contemporary systems of education. In the case of literary education, which deals with texts which may themselves have mystified or demystified historical events and social relationships, the teacher/critic's role in shaping understanding is especially crucial, for in addition to propagating methods of interpreting texts he also decides which texts should be interpreted. I shall return later to the way in which criticism can operate as an agent of mystification, and shall also discuss a number of propagandistic literary texts. But first we must examine one further aspect of the literary process, namely the situation in which a reader attributes to a text meanings which he considers to be totally natural and spontaneous, but which may in fact derive from an interpretant which is itself the product of integration propaganda.

4

The integrated reader

A basic model of communication which could be applied both to literature and propaganda is as follows:

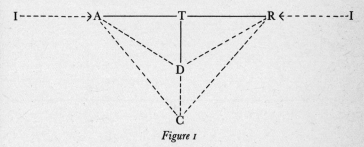

Figure 1

In this model, A is the author, who produces the text (T) which is received by the reader (R). The text is taken to be a structure of signs which possess designative values (D), while the designata can themselves possess connotative dimensions (C). The lines which run from D and C to both A and R are broken in order to indicate that the designata and connotations perceived or intended by A are not necessarily identical to those perceived by R. In some cases, of course, as in the example of a reader confronting a text in a totally unfamiliar language, there may be no shared perception at all; or the reader might wrongly identify the language, reading e.g. the Latin 'i vitelli dei romani

sono belli' as if it were Italian (Eco 1977, p. 140). The relationship which obtains between R and D/C and A and
D/C, finally, is subject to the controlling influence of I, which
represents the interpretant(s) in the broadest sense, including
ultimately the individual experience of the multifarious ideological and social forces which modify, shape and suggest our
understanding of all signs. The relationship between D and C, and
the influence of I on the reader's perception of C, are especially relevant to an analysis of propaganda, for they are
deeply involved with the reader's politically or socially desirable
'correct' understanding of the realities or values conveyed or
able to be conveyed by the text.

Schools of criticism, which in Morris's sense function as
'descriptions of aspects of a complex process' claiming to be
'rival accounts of the whole process', distort the model by
introducing hierarchies of interpretants, the purpose of which is
often to create rules regarding validation procedures, admissi-
bility of evidence and so on. Interestingly, twentieth-century
criticism has moved steadily across the model from left to right;
biographical emphasis was dislodged by various text-related
methods such as New Criticism, while more recently these
methods have been replaced by a criticism based on reader-
response. This process is by no means absolute, however, for we
can usually be sure that just as one theorist announces the
'Death of the Author' as the 'Absolute Subject of Literature'
(Belsey 1980, p. 134), someone else is arguing for a 'logical
connection between statements about the meaning of a literary
work and statements about the author's intention such that a
statement about the meaning of a work *is* a statement about the
author's intention' (Juhl 1980, p. 12).

Quite apart from these more or less established methods of
interpretation, about which more will be said later, there is a
sense in which texts seem to be capable of interpreting themselves, naturally, innocently, without apparent intervention. A
celebrated example is provided by Roland Barthes in his essay
Myth Today. Discussing the cover photograph of an issue of
Paris-Match, which depicted a young black soldier in French
uniform, eyes uplifted, probably saluting the French flag,
Barthes went on to suggest that the deeper significance of the
picture was that 'France is a great empire . . . all her sons,

without any colour discrimination, faithfully serve under her flag . . . and there is no better answer to the detractors of an alleged colonialism than the zeal shown by this negro in serving his so-called oppressors' (Barthes 1972, p. 116). Within the semiological system expounded by Barthes in *Myth Today*, the deeper significance he describes is an example of 'mythical speech' (Barthes 1972, p. 115) which occurs when the 'sign' (i.e. the meaning) of a primary set of signifiers slips straight into a secondary system of signification where it functions as a new signifier. Barthes's formal account of this process is enlightening and attractively simple, and in a certain sense it is true that his analysis 'begins to take us "behind the scene" as it were of our own construction of the world' (Hawkes 1977, p. 133). Yet when we look more closely at Barthes's analysis of the photograph, it becomes clear that his own metacritical perspective is itself in need of explanation, for he is speaking not of a dual sign process consisting of meaning and mythical signification, but of a three-dimensional system which includes his own recognition of mythical signification. Using the model discussed above (p. 29), we might depict the process as in Figure 2 overleaf.

Barthes's ability to 'see through' the process of secondary signification derives from a set of reception interpretants which transform him into the observer of an act of communication which presupposes a different set of interpretants. His own non-conformist position, in other words, has led him to postulate and reject a larger societal inclination towards national pride and its symbols. His interpretation is based on both a recognition and a repudiation of the interpretants, not on a blindness to them. Within his own society he has created for himself a cultural-historical perspective which might serve as a base for what Eco has called 'semiotic guerilla warfare' (Eco 1977, p. 150), an activity which would involve 'a *tactic* of decoding where the message as expression form does not change but the addressee rediscovers his *freedom of decoding*' (Eco 1977, p. 150). But such a tactic can become a truly effective method of analysis only if we assume that the *Paris-Match* picture is operating as vertical political propaganda, if we assume in other words that a wicked colonialist editor or photographer is manipulating images in order to dupe an innocent readership, and that an act of criticism can unmask

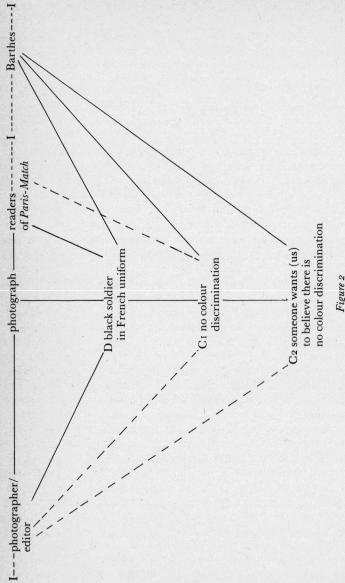

Figure 2

him. If, on the other hand, we view Barthes as a witness of sociological integration propaganda, then it may be that the readers postulated by him are in fact accomplices, not victims. The photograph would then be seen to be reflecting and reinforcing public views, not seeking to modify or transform them in any specific way. The act of demystification will thus be frustrated by the fact that the propagandee 'provokes the psychological action of propaganda, and not merely lends himself to it, but even derives satisfaction from it' (Ellul 1973, p. 121).

The same process can be illustrated by an example taken from contemporary cigarette advertising. In Britain, where the restrictions on cigarette advertising have been stronger than in some other countries (e.g. West Germany), the tobacco companies seemed for a time to be looking mainly for loopholes in the regulations and for alternative methods of promotion which would permit them to continue to advertise cigarettes without admitting each time that they were also selling disease. Sports events were sponsored by well-known brand-names, for example, and TV commercials for pipe tobacco, which are still allowed, were apparently designed so as to promote simultaneously the names of well-known cigarettes. In recent years, however, a more sinister type of advertisement has started to appear which, far from attempting to conceal the relationship between cigarette smoking and death, seems to exploit it in various ways. Pyramids evoke a mood of timeless grandeur; black doors beckon to the dark mystery of the beyond; the golden prize on the sea-bed signifies danger to those who wish to claim it.

Now it may be that the cigarette manufacturers employed motivational researchers to find out why people continued to smoke in spite of health warnings, and that the result of such an investigation suggested that smokers, like many people recurrently involved in accidents, were responding to a subconscious death-wish. Artists were then engaged to transform this death-wish into a series of attractive images. All this could have happened, but I think it more likely that the process whereby the health warning became a selling point emerged gradually as a kind of unconscious conspiracy between smokers and advertisers, an act of horizontal integration propaganda in which both authors and receivers were responding to the same set of interpretants.

In the terms of linguistics, we might say that integration propaganda can act as a situational context which determines the significance of texts. This significance may be related to authorial intention, and equally it may be signalled by interpretants which have been structured into the text. But it is also important to recognize that the significance may derive wholly from the horizon of expectations provided by the receivers, and in this case there may not necessarily be a contradiction between critics who state that we must observe 'what books actually say', and those who declare that the text 'is not the issuing source of meaning'. Even texts which have been intended and structured so as to elicit a certain type of response can be assimilated into signifying patterns which may serve to politicize or to depoliticize the message. In 1941, when a Zurich reviewer admired Brecht's play *Mother Courage* as a 'deeply moving portrayal of the vitality of the maternal animal' (Hecht 1964, p. 165), he was probably reflecting the understanding of an integrated audience rather than trying to create it. In the terms of integrated propaganda, he was acting to restore the very modes of perception which the play had threatened to shatter, but it is doubtful he could have succeeded without the collaboration of the Zurich audience. Integration thus becomes a process capable even of producing the meanings and realities necessary to its own perpetuation.

The integrated reader's need for self-mystification, together with his ability to conceal from himself the process whereby he satisfies the need, is depicted succinctly in Franz Kafka's short piece *Up in the Gallery* (Kafka 1961, pp. 144–5). The story consists of two paragraphs, both of which portray the perception of a circus performance and the behaviour which might be provoked by each perception. The first vision, presented as a hypothesis, begins,

If some frail, consumptive equestrienne in the circus were to be urged round and round . . . for months on end without respite by a ruthless ringmaster . . . and if this performance were likely to continue in the infinite perspective of a drab future to the unceasing roar of the orchestra and hum of the

> ventilators, accompanied by ebbing and renewed swelling
> bursts of applause which are really steam hammers

then, the paragraph concludes, 'perhaps, a young visitor to the
gallery might race down the long stairs through all the circles,
rush into the ring, and yell: Stop! against the fanfares of the
orchestra still playing the appropriate music' (Kafka 1961,
p. 144). The second paragraph, which uses in German the in-
dicative mood of reality rather than the subjunctive of unreality
employed in the first description, reintegrates the picture for
us:

> But since that is not so; a lovely lady, pink and white, floats in
> between the curtains. . . . Since that is so, the visitor to the
> gallery lays his face on the rail before him and, sinking into
> the closing march as into a heavy dream, weeps without
> knowing it. (Kafka 1961, p. 145)

If literature can express this insight, does it follow that art can
actively demystify, can catch the forces of integration unawares
as it were, and induce a moment of self-reflection, however
brief? Kafka himself certainly thought so, for when once asked
to comment on the difference between run-of-the-mill writing
and real literature, he stated that whereas the former was
essentially soporific in effect, the true function of the latter was
to 'awaken' (Janouch 1961, p. 64). Recent critical practice,
which has attempted to reconstitute itself as a system for
liberating the reader, for transforming him into a 'producer of
meaning' rather than a consumer of texts (Belsey 1980, pp.
125ff.), can thus be seen as a kind of second-level 'semiotic
guerilla warfare'. For even though there are countless works of
literature which, in Kafka's sense, mythify, mystify and 'put us
to sleep', there are also texts which 'awaken', and which express
their capacity to do so in a manner which makes critical
assistance redundant.

A case in point, which can serve to conclude this part of the
discussion, is Yevgeny Zamyatin's novel *We*, which was described in the 1929–30 *Literary Encyclopedia* (Moscow) as 'merely
a disguise for a very matter-of-fact and quite understandable
pining of the bourgeoisie after the economic well-being it has
forfeited' (Rühle 1969, p. 35). The work was banned in the

Soviet Union, however, presumably because not all readers could be relied on to understand it in this way. In fact, Zamyatin, who had at first enthusiastically supported the Bolshevik revolution, presents in his novel a perfectly integrated, ant-like society governed by a code of laws, the Tables of Hourly Commandments, which plan to the second the daily lives of the inhabitants of The One State. An engineer by training, Zamyatin was able to incorporate into his novel a plausible account of how technology would come to be used in order to regiment humanity and programme its 'happiness'. The One State is none the less not perfectly self-contained, for it is separated from the 'wild plains' by a Green Wall, from beyond which anarchy and potential subversion may drift in with the wind:

> From beyond the Green Wall, from the wild plains that lie out of sight, the wind brings the honeyed yellow pollen of certain flowers. The lips become dry from this pollen; you run your tongue over them every minute or so, and, in all probability, all the women you come across have sweet lips now. . . . This interferes with logical thinking, to some extent. (Zamyatin 1924, p. 169; Rühle 1969, p. 39)

Quite apart from its function in the novel, the above passage from *We* touches upon the broader political and social significance of art and literature. The 'sweetness' of art, Zamyatin seems to suggest, far from being a mere accompaniment to the didactic content of an *utile cum dulce* literature, is itself capable of modifying the individual's relationship to the official truths of his society. We will return later to this concept of art as demystification.

5
Linguistic determinism and literary freedom

There is a point of view known as linguistic determinism which has been associated variously with the writings of Wilhelm von Humboldt, Edward Sapir, Benjamin Whorf, Emile Durkheim and, more recently, of L. S. Vygotsky (Lyons 1968, pp. 432ff.; Cherry 1978, pp. 306ff.; Eco 1977, pp. 76ff.). The so-called Sapir-Whorf hypothesis, which represents the extreme form of linguistic determinism, holds that language does not reflect 'reality', but rather creates it according to the structures and limits permitted by the language of a given culture: in Sapir's words, 'we see and hear and otherwise experience very largely as we do because the language habits of our community predispose certain choices of interpretation' (Whorf 1956, p. 134).

Observing how linguistic factors could predominate over obvious physical ones (Whorf 1956, pp. 135ff.), and at the same time investigating the expressive possibilities of non-Indoeuropean languages, Whorf spoke of a 'linguistically determined thought world' which 'not only collaborates with our cultural idols and ideals, but engages even our unconscious reactions in its patterns and gives them certain typical characters' (Whorf 1956, p. 154). Each language ordains the forms and categories by which we not only communicate, but also analyse the external world, notice or neglect relationships and phenomena, channel reasoning and build 'the house of consciousness' (Whorf 1956, p. 252). The mind, in short, uses language in order to 'make a provisional analysis of reality and then regard it as final', and 'Western culture has gone farthest here, farthest in determined thoroughness of provisional analysis, and farthest in determination to regard it as final' (Whorf 1956, p. 263).

Even if we accept this view, or a modified form of it known as 'cultural relativity' (Lyons 1968, p. 433), it does not follow that the limits of individual consciousness or the capacity for unorthodox thought are permanently imprisoned, any more than the Marxist premise that 'being determines consciousness' implies inevitable human passivity. As Solomon suggests, the premise should be understood as 'the dialectical twin of the proposition that "men make their own history"' (Solomon 1979, p. 17). The limits of consciousness may co-terminate with the boundaries of language, but these boundaries are in a constant state of flux and redefinition. Even states like Nazi Germany, which made a systematic effort to control public and private consciousness by controlling language, found that their extraordinarily detailed directives concerning language usage could swiftly be subverted by popular processes. When Goering ill-advisedly claimed that he would be called Meier (i.e. 'I'm a Dutchman') if a single bomb fell on Germany, it was not long before the air-raid sirens in the Ruhr were referred to locally as 'Meier's French horn' (Balfour 1979, p. 433). Ritualized laughter of this kind, as Mikhail Bakhtin has persuasively argued, can serve to dissolve authoritarian commandments and clarify consciousness; it liberates not only from external censorship, but 'first of all from the great interior censor' (Bakhtin 1979, pp. 298, 300).

Language is none the less part of the 'great interior censor', and the acquisition of language must be regarded as the first and most significant stage in the process of socialization whereby the individual assimilates the modes of perception and value systems which determine his own historicity. Language is thus the first source of integration propaganda for the individual, and to the extent that its acquisition leads a person to believe that his individuality is an essence, to be expressed through language, rather than the product of a given culture, it will have succeeded in playing its first trick.

Cultural and linguistic identity do not however imply cultural homogeneity, for as Emile Durkheim has pointed out, even though an individual and his language are products of a society and culture, there exist poles of 'mechanical solidarity' and 'organic solidarity'; societies where no disagreement of any kind would be tolerated as opposed to societies whose existence depends on a network of acknowledged differences (Cherry 1978, p. 308). A language like Afrikaans would typify the one direction, while English, which now reflects and expresses a number of quite divergent cultures, is characteristic of the latter. James Booth has demonstrated how post-colonial African writers, who had every reason to distance themselves from linguistically induced consciousness, were able to 'subvert and refashion English in the attempt to express themselves authentically' (Booth 1981, p. 66). In recent years North American Indian writers (e.g. Scott Mommaday, Leslie Silko, James Welch) have similarly used English as a vehicle for introducing fresh concepts and realities into the American consciousness, and in doing so they have not merely discarded the stereotypes of 'noble savage' or 'dangerous savage', but have succeeded in creating new sets of interpretants. Once these interpretants become current they can readily be applied to other situations, and thus a rejection of the Indian-killer as cultural hero can produce a rejection of the US Marine in Vietnam as national hero. Fiction, in other words, can provide us with the interpretants necessary to see through the second-level semiological process which Barthes described as mythical speech.

In his discussion of linguistic determinism, Eco points out that 'within a given culture a semantic field can disintegrate with extreme rapidity and restructure itself into a new field' (Eco 1977, p. 80), and he suggests that the interesting task from the semiotic point of view is to 'understand within which civilizations a semantic field functions and at what point it begins to dissolve in order to make room for another' (Eco 1977, p. 79). It seems to me that some recent critics of ideology overlook the fact that this process of rapid disintegration is synchronic; it can be observed to be happening within the structure of a language at a given time.

Terry Eagleton is probably right when he states that in cases where authorial ideologies are in conflict with a dominant general ideology, 'their modes of ideological disinheritance from their historical moment are determined, in the last instance, by the nature of that moment itself' (Eagleton 1976, p. 59). On the other hand he surely underestimates the capacity of fiction to subvert the very processes of general ideology, and not merely to express its sense of disinheritance from it. He describes *Bleak House* as signifying 'not Victorian England' as such, but 'certain of Victorian England's ways of signifying itself' (Eagleton 1976, p. 77); *The Heart of Darkness* similarly presents a 'viewpoint which disturbs imperialist assumptions to the precise degree that it reinforces them' (Eagleton 1976, p. 135). The point is not that Conrad's novel can be interpreted as a more powerful condemnation of imperialism (cf. Dolan 1976, pp. 98ff.), but that Eagleton seems to be denying fiction the same degree of detachment from a culturally determined position that was being claimed by contemporary writers of non-fiction. If *The Heart of Darkness* reinforces imperialistic assumptions 'to the precise degree' that it questions them, and if this degree is a function of the inevitable entanglement of fiction with the general ideology it seeks to question, then fiction is a weak substitute for such critical works as J. A. Hobson's *The Psychology of Jingoism* (1901, London). For Hobson recognized clearly what Eagleton permits Conrad only to half-see, namely that the 'Jingo spirit . . . disables a nation from getting outside itself' (cf. Raskin 1967, pp. 109–27).

As recent studies of racism and sexism in language have demonstrated, ideology can function within language as integration propaganda, and can in consequence socialize speakers to the point that they are oblivious of having been socialized: 'The power of the fathers has been difficult to grasp because it permeates everything, even the language in which we try to describe it' (Rich 1977, p. 41). Such power has none the less been described, if only because 'it is in language that the ideology inscribed in the language can be challenged' (Belsey 1980, p. 44). The power of language to construct a particular social reality can be challenged in fiction precisely because of fiction's ability not merely to question analytically, but to present through language a totally different vision of possible social formations. Just as *Nineteen-Eighty-Four* uses language in order to warn against the ultimate propagandized society, other futuristic novels portray quite different political and linguistic utopias. Carol Pearson, in a recent study of feminist utopian fiction, shows how works by Dorothy Bryant and Mary Staton depict a transition from 'a primitive, linear mode of consciousness, marked by internal repression and external oppression, to a more complex, multiple mode of thinking that results from the integration of thought and feeling' (Pearson 1981, p. 130). Mary Staton's novel *From the Legend of Biel* (1975, New York) postulates a future anarchistic society which will emerge from a revolutionary transformation of language. Before the non-violent revolution,

> sickness was manifest in and encouraged (in) language . . . these ill people spoke of owning each other, of owning land, ideas, animals, everything. They permitted governments and systems to try and control nonexistent entities like The People, Education, Health, even Death. (Staton, quoted by Pearson 1981, p. 131)

With reference to the definitions of propaganda and communication so far discussed, it might be fruitful at this point to consider the methods through which propaganda might reassert itself when challenged by a work of fiction. Moving across the Author – Text – Reader model given above, we find that we are in fact moving from authoritarian vertical propaganda towards a process of horizontal integration propaganda. The totalitarian state, which frequently attempts to impose 'correct' political interpretants by edict, can usually be expected to act swiftly against authors and texts which might seem to be smuggling deviant interpretants into the sign process. Authors are then imprisoned, silenced, 'rehabilitated' in psychiatric clinics, or forced to rewrite the offending text. Texts likewise will be suppressed or rewritten, if not by the author then by the censor.

One of the more bizarre features of this type of control is that the authoritarian state may itself decide on a new set of interpretants, with the result that texts may have to be rewritten more than once. An example is Fyodor Gladkov's novel *Cement*, widely circulated in the Soviet Union as a model for the novels of industrial construction written in the 1930s. In the first edition of *Cement* (1925) the hero Gleb addresses the proletarian crowd with the words, 'The blood and suffering of the battle – these are our weapons for winning the whole world'. But by 1950 the speech had been transformed into: 'We are building our own world with our own hands. With the name of Lenin on our lips, with faith in unlimited happiness let us double and treble our efforts for the conquest of the future' (Brown 1969, pp. 169–70).

In less authoritarian societies the process of control is different but often no less effective; it derives from the existing interpretants of integration propaganda which have the power to nullify the challenge or to absorb it into a familiar pattern of signification. And in a very important sense, integration propaganda rewrites dissident literature, sometimes quite literally.

The more obvious instances of this occur when a written work, usually a 'modern classic', is transferred to the screen. Friedrich Dürrenmatt's play *Der Besuch der alten Dame* was provided with a quite different ending when it was filmed as *The Visit*, starring Anthony Quinn and Ingrid Bergman. Superficially, it might be thought that the fact that Alfred Ill does not die in the film version was a straightforward example of Hollywood giving in to the box-office demand for a happy ending. The scriptwriters were giving the public what it wanted. Yet the real dissonance of Dürrenmatt's play is not that Ill dies – Hollywood has devised countless methods for resolving the dissonance of a hero's death – but that a community can decide by majority democratic vote to murder one of its members for profit. In the film version of the play integration propaganda can thus be seen diverting attention from one of its own contradictions: the equation of democracy with individual liberty. The process by which 'limited-appeal' art is refashioned into mass culture is illuminating, for it offers one of the few vantage-points from which contemporary integration may be observed.

Sometimes integration propaganda does not need to rewrite the counter-visions of reality which threaten to subvert it; it merely overpowers them by marshalling its own preferred interpretants. Nathanael West's novel *A Cool Million*, which supposedly exposed the Horatio Alger myth of poor-boy-makes-good, is still submerged in a flood of TV drama, popular fiction and newspaper stories of the 'Penniless Greek Immigrant Dies a Millionaire' variety. More often, however, the potentially subversive interpretant is juxtaposed with existing ones in such a way that it becomes impoverished as a source of new meaning. The concept of woman as sex-object gives rise to art forms and news reports which treat the liberated woman as sex-object. Mary Ellmann, the authoress of *Thinking About Women*, is introduced in her book as 'living in Oxford, where her husband is Goldsmiths' Professor of English Literature'. The American Indian, once he has established his complete humanity, is permitted to kill on a vast scale in his own right, and thus participates in the 'myth of regeneration through violence . . . the structuring metaphor of the American experience' (Slotkin 1973, p. 5).

Perhaps the most powerful weapon in the arsenal of integration propaganda is what George Szanto has called 'content distortion'. Szanto (1978, pp. 28–37) describes five basic categories of distortion, the largest and least explicable of which is a

> totally self-consistent, easily acceptable message. . . . This is content distortion . . . it creates a *total sense of consistent reality* which to the nonanalytic mind (itself the desired product of content distortion) becomes the very essence of realism. . . . Often the necessary language for the analysis of a piece of content distortion will itself be integrated into the message of the distortion. (Szanto 1978, p. 36)

The film *Easy Rider* is cited as an example. The film purports to be discussing and even celebrating the alternative life-styles and subcultures which arose in the United States in the late 1960s. In fact, it states that integrated society still has its boundaries, which now include certain types of subculture, beyond which there is neither a return nor a future. 'We blew it', says one of the characters, expressing his own knowledge of the film's real message: 'that young men who reject institutionalized society cannot escape it and so will be killed by the least of human elements in that society' (Szanto 1978, p. 36).

For reasons which will be discussed later, integration propaganda in western societies is no longer the powerful force within literature that it used to be. To some extent this is also true of film, despite the above examples. Its real operational base is now to be found in television and other mass media, including the popular press. This does not mean that this type of propaganda has vanished from literature, but simply that the literary text is no longer the most effective vehicle for its transmission and perpetuation. The interpretants required in order to control a potentially subversive literary text, i.e. to prevent it from precipitating the sort of semantic disintegration mentioned earlier, must appear to be natural and spontaneous; they must derive from and be reinforced by regular linguistic experience, to which the reading of literary texts now contributes only marginally. Recent empirical work has revealed that not even students specializing in literature read poetry of their own accord, while an investigation into the reading habits of French conscripts, undertaken by Robert Escarpit, showed that of a sample group of almost 5000 three-fifths could not produce the name of a single author (Sammons 1977, p. 101). This was not always the case, however, and a brief look at the way in which literature has functioned traditionally as integration propaganda might yield some insights capable of further application.

6
Capitalist integration myths

Whereas the acquisition of language can be regarded as the first stage of socialization, literature historically belongs to the secondary agencies of socialization which introduce the individual to the schemes of interpretation dominant in his society. Language produces the awareness of a world which can be touched by words, and literature seemingly develops and refines this awareness by using words in order to explore the newly unfolding reality.

The common justification for literature, both as a leisure activity and as part of the educational system, is that it 'expands the vision', and while it would be pointless to deny that certain works of fiction can achieve this, or something like it, we must also recognize that fiction is equally capable of reducing the vision. Children's literature, the first encounters with which are still deeply and often consciously involved with language acquisition, has proved itself historically to be a crucial element in the process of socialization. We may pay lip-service to the undifferentiated childlike vision which fails to see the emperor's new clothes, but from the industrial revolution to the present we have produced countless works for children which suppress the potential anarchy of such a vision by introducing and reinforcing the desired modes of perceiving and responding (i.e. the interpretants) to the emperor's power.

In his penetrating study of children's literature and bourgeois ideology, Isaac Kramnick shows how the great integration myths of industrial capitalism were introduced into literature in the later eighteenth century. They were exemplified in such works as Thomas Day's *Little Jack* (1786), which can be seen as a precursor of twentieth-century stories like Mabel C. Bragg's *The Little Engine That Could*, which has sold more than five million copies since its first appearance in 1926. Both stories illustrate the success which follows the acceptance of the individualist ethos, the belief that hard work, the will to achieve and dogged independence will bring material rewards. Part of Kramnick's thesis is that the industrial revolution, by providing the economic basis for a 'private and nuclear family' (Kramnick 1980, p. 210), introduced new concepts of childhood and motherhood which separated women and children from the processes of production. This created leisure hours which might be filled by reading (aloud) works which glorified the industrial revolution and the bourgeois engineers and scientists whose efforts had made it possible. The books which responded to this new family structure were at first openly and vigorously didactic. For the most part they devised fictional scenes capable of driving home direct messages almost as straightforward as the exhortations of Josiah Wedgwood's *An Address to the young Inhabitants of the Pottery* (1783, Newcastle), which praised the virtues of frugality, thrift, respect for machines, productivity, temperateness and so on.

Attitudes towards the acquisition of wealth were ambivalent, for on the one hand virtue would inevitably be rewarded by financial success, and on the other the hero or heroine (cf. *The History of Little Goody Two-Shoes*, 1765) must never be permitted to be seduced by wealth. The bourgeoisie, in other words, had to establish its moral superiority over the aristocracy, whose dominant position it was challenging.

Just one of the many themes discussed by Kramnick – a theme which still recurs regularly in popular films – is the power of the English and American bourgeoisie to reward its own virtues when it encounters them in unlikely places, e.g. abroad. Maria Edgeworth's *The Little Merchants* relates the astonishment of a group of English tourists when they encounter an honest street-trader in Naples. Young Francisco is paid the ultimate compliment: 'Bless you my good boy, I should have taken you for an Englishman by your ways of dealing' (Kramnick 1980, p.

222). Francisco is taken back to England, where he earns his reward and, it might be added, confirms another English prejudice by becoming an artist.

Perhaps the most interesting work discussed by Kramnick is Maria Edgeworth's *Harry and Lucy* (2 vols, 1825), which he describes as 'a hymn to science and industry and the godlike figures who have made England what it was in the 1790s, the factory of the world' (p. 222). The work is significant not only for the detail with which the industrial revolution and its socioeconomic effects is presented and praised, but also on account of the implications concerning class and sex differences. When Harry and Lucy are taken on holiday, the tourist sights are not castles and cathedrals ('the past'), but potteries, steel factories, steam engines, etc. The visit to a steel mill is portrayed as follows:

> half smouldering heaps of coal, clouds of smoke of all colours, from the chimneys and foundries and forges. The hands and faces of everyone were covered with soot. Lucy said it was the most frightful country she had ever beheld. Harry acknowledged that there was nothing beautiful here to be seen; but it was wonderful, it was a sort of sublime. He could not help feeling a great respect for the place, where steam engines seemed to abound, and in truth, to have the world almost to themselves. (Kramnick 1980, p. 223)

Lucy's sense of fright is of course appropriate to a future domestic role which will isolate her from the means of production. But what of the wives and families of those whose hands and faces were 'covered with soot'? The reader's possible curiosity is both anticipated and forestalled a few pages later in a scene which describes how Harry and Lucy are taken by the factory manager to the home of one of the workers. Just as they arrive, the man is beating his wife, and immediately afterwards Harry and Lucy see that the woman and her children wait on the worker with great servility. When the visiting children ask the manager why he has not intervened, he explains that he has no right to take such action, for 'every man has the liberty to do as he pleases in his own home and in his own affairs'. Kramnick writes of the passage: 'This is liberal freedom. It is crowning the

new bourgeois home and family structure with the sanctity of
laissez-faire ideology' (Kramnick 1980, p. 225).

Kramnick's critical method, which analyses the ideological
content of fiction by relating it to historical background and
documentary materials, provides numerous insights into the
way in which industrial capitalism used literature as a means of
disseminating the interpretants necessary to its survival. From
the perspective of propaganda, however, we need to investigate
this process not merely as a reduplication of static exemplary
myths but as a fluid and dynamic source of persuasion capable
of adapting itself to whatever position capitalism may have to
defend. Our own historicity as readers, which to a large extent
permits us to understand the points made by Kramnick, must
be incorporated into a method with which we approach contemporary as well as past texts. The conflicts and contradictions
visible in earlier texts, moreover, need to be seen as possibly
permanent structural aspects of capitalism and not just as
time-bound examples of its unacceptable face. The wife-beating
scene in *Harry and Lucy*, for instance, reveals one of the continuing contradictions of bourgeois ideology precisely by trying
to conceal it. Like the doors which swing open in the fiction of
Franz Kafka to allow a disconcerting glimpse of a horrifying
reality which somehow coexists with 'normal life', the curtains
in *Harry and Lucy* part briefly to permit a prurient and guilty
readership to observe a proletarian sub-world which stands in
contrast to the values which the novel celebrates. But that
sub-world is also a grotesque parody of those values, seen as it is
in terms of the overriding principle which states that 'every man
has the liberty to do as he pleases in his own home'.

Later children's fiction, serving the demands of most post-
revolutionary periods, gave up the preaching tone in favour of
a literature which presented the new social order as the
permanent and natural way to organize industrial society. The
requirements of industrial capitalism, including the division
of labour, economic inequality and the absolute sanctity of private property, manifested themselves as changeless features of
human existence. The class system produced by capitalism was
rendered innocuous by the myth that the ambitious individual
still had the capacity to relocate himself within the appointed
structure of power and prosperity. Although a number of

educational acts and industrial reforms provided for a growing base of literacy among the children of the workers, the reading matter available to them was not likely to contribute to a deeper understanding of social and economic relationships. The educational system, itself widely interpreted as the ladder of upward mobility provided by a benevolent society, introduced children to the moral and social values considered desirable by a dominant class, while popular fiction of the Boys' and Girls' Library variety portrayed a world in which the children of this class were seen at work and play. The trappings of this fictional world – rich aunts, exciting vacations, country houses, mysterious presents, private schools, etc. – might seem to be the innocent expression of a bourgeoisie indulging itself after its successful revolution. Yet on a deeper level these recurrent motifs and milieus were able to operate as powerful integrating factors. The insidious aspect for a working-class child reading such fiction was not that it depicted a world from which he was excluded, but that its particular settings and situations, like those of the fictive aristocratic world which it had replaced, suggested that authentic feeling and genuine freedom were possible only within this setting. The desire to enter this class and thereby to become a 'real person' was gratified by various Cinderella myths in which the eccentric prince is banished in favour of bourgeois talent-spotters.

A recurrent and interesting feature of capitalist integration literature, where it sometimes seems to become conscious of itself as an aspect of integration, lies in the role it assigns to language. As a highly complex structure of social agreement concerning usage, meaning and sound, language can become a metaphor for the intricate rules and combinatory relationships which determine the position of the individual vis-à-vis society. 'Correct speech' as an indicator of social status was parodied in Shaw's well-known account of Eliza Doolittle in *Pygmalion* (1914), and a great deal of amusement derives from the possibility of phonetic deception around which the plot of the play revolves. The socializing power of language can however appear at a much deeper level, and can function even in works intended for very young children as a potent secondary myth capable of reinforcing a primary capitalist one.

An example is Beatrix Potter's charmingly illustrated *Tale of*

Squirrel Nutkin, which describes how a community of squirrels set out each day to gather nuts on an island. Since the island is owned by an owl, Old Mr Brown, the squirrels must have his permission before they can collect food on his property, and so every morning before beginning their own search for food they procure delicacies for the owl in the form of 'fat mice', 'a fine fat mole', 'seven fat minnows', 'wild honey . . . stolen out of a bumble-bees' nest' and so on. These gifts are delivered most respectfully, with each squirrel making a low bow and saying politely, 'Old Mr Brown, will you favour us with permission to gather nuts on your island?' The owl, who spends most of his time sleeping, accepts the food. Squirrel Nutkin, the impudent 'hero' of the tale, will have none of this. Described as having 'no respect', and 'no nice manners', he not only refuses to gather nuts but even has the temerity to dance around Old Mr Brown, teasing him with ingenious riddles and tickling him with a nettle. One day he carries his antics too far and is seized by the owl who 'held him up by the tail, intending to skin him'. At the cost of half his tail, Nutkin manages to escape, and one might expect that by now both he and the young reader will have learned to accept the naturalness of a society in which a land-owning owl sleeps while squirrels work both for themselves and the owl. In fact, the story is more than a simple integration myth, and it remains silent on the question of whether Nutkin became a 'good squirrel', for the fate it had in store for him could not be redeemed by 'respect' and 'nice manners'. On the last page the capitalist myth recedes to make room for the more frightening suggestion that Nutkin, by using his skill with words in a playful and subversive way, has forfeited his right to be integrated into a language community. At the very end, the squirrel who was so brilliant with words and riddles, is capable only of shouting: 'Cuck-cuck-cuck-cur-r-r-cuck-k-k!' In a sense, *The Tale of Squirrel Nutkin* can be seen as an inverted version of Hans Christian Andersen's *The Emperor's New Clothes,* for it invokes undifferentiated pre-linguistic consciousness as a state of isolation into which the individual can be plunged if he or she refuses to use language, the primary mode of perception, as a means of expressing the correct secondary perceptions of the community.

Morgan Evans, the young Welsh hero of Emlyn Williams's

play *The Corn is Green* (first performed 1938; edn referred to here, 1981), learns his linguistic lesson properly and is rewarded with a scholarship to Oxford. His fairy godmother is Miss Moffat, 'a healthy Englishwoman with an honest face, clear, beautiful eyes' (Williams 1981, p. 8), who settles in a remote village in Wales in order to open a school. Evans, described by Miss Moffat as her 'little pit-pony' (Williams 1981, p. 56), writes an essay which reveals a remarkable gift for poetic expression, and he is therefore singled out for individual advancement, the various stages of which become symbols vindicating the school's existence. His education, which begins with a spanking followed by lots of grammar (Williams 1981, pp. 30–4), is presented openly as a socialization process. In Act I he is unwashed and 'truculent' (Williams 1981, p. 30); two years later he has become 'the submissive schoolboy' (Williams 1981, p. 41), and when he bows twice before the Squire, saying, 'Excuse me, sir . . . Good afternoon, sir,' he is even taken for a relative of Miss Moffat (Williams 1981, p. 52). By Act III the transformation is almost complete, and Evans is able to spend half an hour in discussion with the president of an Oxford college, a 'grand old gentleman sitting in a drawing-room the size of Penlan Town Hall' (Williams 1981, p. 79). The effect of Oxford on Evans is described revealingly by him in a scene introduced with the note that his 'English has immensely improved, and he expresses himself with ease' (Williams 1981, p. 79). He explains:

> I have *been* to Oxford, and come back . . . I have come back – from the world! Since the day I was born, I have been a prisoner behind a stone wall, and now somebody has given me a leg-up to have a look at the other side . . . (*vehement*) . . . they cannot drag me back again, they cannot, they *must* give me a push and send me over! (Williams 1981, p. 80)

The relationship between English and Welsh dialogue in the play is a complex one, for the two languages function as far more than a convenient code used to indicate social difference. When Evans expresses his gratitude to Miss Moffat towards the end of the piece, he looks back at his pre-educated state and claims that he had 'a vocabulary of twenty words' (Williams 1981, p. 81). It may seem curious that his knowledge of Welsh is overlooked, for the essay which drew attention to his creative intelligence was an imperfect translation from Welsh. Throughout the play, in fact, Welsh serves as a symbol for pre-individual consciousness; it represents a mysterious and anarchistic realm which can be organized and controlled only through the medium of English. It appears as the language of song and (for the English audience) unintelligible group speech. When Evans is chastised the class expresses its astonishment by falling into a 'quick tangle of Welsh', and 'pandemonium' is signalled by 'a torrent of Welsh imprecations' (Williams 1981, p. 18). Later, when Evans loses his self-control and resists Miss Moffat's authority, his speech is described as 'a rising torrent of invective, getting more Welsh as it goes on' (Williams 1981, p. 47). When Sarah hurries into the school one day, dressed in the 'traditional Welsh peasant costume with a steeple hat', she disrupts the sense of stability by addressing her father in Welsh, but is immediately admonished by 'Old Tom (*furious*): English, daughter, in the class, pliss!' (Williams 1981, p. 75). At a crucial point in the play, Evans's career is threatened by Bessie Watty, an English girl whose mother works for Miss Moffat. Significantly, as Evans perfects his English Bessie begins to learn Welsh, and in the seduction scene she is depicted as a siren-like creature whose destructive charms evoke the mystery and uncontrollable passion of Evans's pre-English consciousness:

> She wanders up towards the bay window, and begins to sing in Welsh, in a voice surprisingly pure and pleasing. The tune is 'Lliw Gwyn Rhosyn yr Haf'. He raises his head and listens, arrested. She leans against one of the desks in the window recess, and looks out towards the setting sun; her voice ends softly on a phrase. (Williams 1981, p. 62)

Bessie is presented generally as a scheming and empty-headed person, a 'guttersnipe species' (Miss Moffat, Williams 1981, p. 46) totally unworthy of Morgan Evans. When she returns to the village with Evans's child, it seems proper that Miss Moffat should adopt the baby so that Evans is not forced to marry and remain in Glansarno as the 'besotted and uncouth village genius' (Williams 1981, pp. 93–4). He is dispatched to Oxford, with hopes of becoming 'a great statesman', and is told by Miss Moffat that 'there is no reason why you should ever come to Glansarno again' (Williams 1981, p. 94).

Had Bessie been a simple Welsh girl, the contradictions surrounding the development of Morgan Evans's 'true' self could not have been resolved with such convincing neatness. Even so, the roles assigned to English and Welsh by the play force it to reveal some of its contradictions even when it attempts to conceal them. An early example is afforded by the Squire, who mistakenly assumes that mass education could lead to subversion:

> They jabber away in that funny lingo, but bless their hearts, it's a free country! But puttin' 'em up to read English, and pothooks, and givin' 'em ideas – if there were more people like you, y'know, England'd be a jolly dangerous place to live in! (Williams 1981, p. 27)

Miss Moffat seems to bear out the Squire's interpretation, for when it becomes clear that he has succeeded in preventing her from acquiring a school building, she confronts him indignantly:

> I should just like to point out that there is a considerable amount of dirt, ignorance, misery and discontent abroad in this world, and that a good deal of it is due to people like you, because you are a stupid, conceited, greedy good-for-nothing, addle-headed nincompoop. (Williams 1981, p. 27)

Miss Moffat appears to be 'dangerous' because the crisis precipitated by the Squire makes her revert to the propaganda of agitation with which the bourgeoisie had rationalized its replacing the aristocracy as the dominant class. Her attack on the landed gentry, and the suggestion that Morgan Evans had to be protected and guided by people like herself, deflects attention from the exploitative relationship which existed between workers and her own class. Her role as an agent of socialization on behalf of this class is contradictory, however, and on one occasion she betrays her knowledge that the education of Morgan Evans is designed to limit his thinking rather than liberate it. Musing on his prospects for the scholarship, she states on the one hand that, 'It depends on how much the examiners will appreciate a highly original intelligence', but on the other, 'If he checks himself, and does not start telling them what they ought to think of Milton, with fair luck he might stand a chance' (Williams 1981, p. 65). Evans has learned to 'check himself', as we hear later from his own account of the examination: 'Parnell . . . Oh yes – I was going to stick up for the old chap, but when they started off with "that fellow Parnell", I told the tale against him for half an hour, I wasn't born a Welshman for nothing' (Williams 1981, p. 79). Perhaps not.

7

Demystification

Demystification is commonly held to be a Marxist strategy which permits us to observe the origins and nature of 'false consciousness'. The theories of economic determinism expounded by Marx and Engels postulated a social superstructure deriving from an economic base. To the extent that the base was a system of unequal economic relationships, the superstructure produced by it, including false consciousness, acted to conceal the true nature of the base and to alienate the individual from the forces which determined his social existence.

Within the history of ideas, and especially within the framework of nineteenth-century German thought, this particular aspect of Marxism can be seen as a variant form of the search for the *Ding-an-sich* (the 'thing-in-itself') which stretches from Kant through Schopenhauer to Freud. The common denominator is the belief that, although we have immediate access only to a world of appearances or phenomena, certain conceptual systems will illuminate the real relationship between phenomena and underlying reality. Unfortunately, such systems tend to attract disciples whose mechanical application of the new interpretive schemes gradually erodes and sometimes even perverts the explanatory power of the original insight. In this respect it is instructive to assess Marx and Freud as literary critics against the body of Marxist and Freudian criticism which purports to carry on their work.

Maynard Solomon has attacked the 'sociogenetic reductionism' of much Marxist criticism, arguing that

> art is itself (like Marxism) a strategy of demystification, a withdrawal from the negative reality of an alienated class society into a different order of reality which common sense deems illusion but which is actually the symbolic precipitate of the material-sensuous substructure of human relations and desires. (Solomon 1979, p. 20)

He proceeds to develop the point:

> Art is a distinct form of the labour process in which – amid the myriad effusions and narcotic productions of class culture – is kept alive the materialized imagery of man's hope and of that very same human essence which Marxism seeks to reveal. (Solomon 1979, p. 20)

In effect, Solomon is arguing here for demystification as both a Marxist and an aesthetic category; his distinction between real art and 'narcotic productions' recalls Kafka's apolitical definition of literature as a force which 'awakens'. A demystifying art, however, is by its nature a subversive and questioning art. It challenges habits and modes of perception, and produces new ways of seeing and interpreting processes and relationships. To do this successfully, it must be unpredictable, surprising, even shocking, and it must be inventive enough to avoid being submerged by an integration propaganda which will naturalize its techniques in the guise of reproducing them. When we begin to look for examples of such art, in Marxist as well as capitalist societies, we encounter a number of apparent paradoxes and contradictions which shed light on, and can in turn be illuminated by, the workings of propaganda.

The leading theorists of demystification were the Russian Formalist Victor Shklovsky, whose seminal essay on *Art as Technique* appeared in 1917, and the German poet and dramatist Bertolt Brecht, whose theoretical and creative writings span a quarter of a century beginning in the early 1920s. Shklovsky, whose formulations bear an interesting resemblance to certain art theories of English Romanticism (Scholes 1974, pp. 83–5, 173–6), is mainly concerned with the way in which art rearranges perception so as to dissolve the familiar but arbitrary

structures of what we regard as reality; art breaks down 'habi-
tualization', which 'devours works, clothes, furniture, one's
wife, and the fear of war (Shklovsky 1965, p. 12). Art 'defamilia-
rizes', and it does so by removing objects 'from the automatism
of perception in several ways' (Shklovsky 1965, p. 13).

He goes on to discuss numerous examples of defamiliarization in literature, ranging from Tolstoy's 'method of seeing
things out of their normal context' (Shklovsky 1965, p. 17), to
the use of unexpected erotic imagery in the *Decameron* (Shklovsky 1965, p. 21) and the introduction of archaisms or dialect
forms into the language of poetry (Shklovsky 1965, pp. 22–3).
Although Shklovsky is chiefly interested in perception as a
general phenomenon, some of his examples make it clear that a
method of 'seeing things out of their normal context' possesses
political and social implications. He comments in some detail
on Tolstoy's horse/narrator in *Kholstomer*, and shows how the
institution of private property is defamiliarized by being presented from the perspective of a horse (Shklovsky 1965, pp.
13–15). Other instances are Tolstoy's way of 'pricking the
conscience' by defamiliarizing society's methods of punishing
criminals (Shklovsky 1965, p. 13) and his 'technique in describing battles as if battles were something new' (Shklovsky 1965, p.
15). This aspect of Russian Formalism is significant, not only
because it contradicts the common view that the movement
chose 'a technical, scientific approach to literature which . . .
ultimately would dehumanize art and destroy criticism' (Wellek 1976, p. 47), but also and especially because it provides the
theoretical and aesthetic basis for an experimental and subversive art.

In retrospect, it is easy to see that later Soviet aesthetics,
which championed Socialist Realism and used the word 'formalism' as a term of abuse, were more concerned to suppress the
notion of art as a destabilizing influence than to crush an elitist
and intellectualized critical method. Writing in 1925 on the
relationship between defamiliarization and artistic motivation,
Boris Tomashevsky seems to be anticipating the growing trend
towards a conformist and integrated art and to be warning
against its basically conservative nature: 'The old, tradition-
orientated group generally denies the artistry of the new literary
form' (Tomashevsky 1965, p. 85).

In contrast to Shklovsky, Brecht developed his theory of the alienation-effect and his concept of the epic theatre precisely as a means of political demystification. His descriptions of aesthetic estrangement frequently resemble those of the Russian Formalists, however, and like them he recognized its universal character. 'The A-effect', he wrote, 'consists in turning the object of which one is to be made aware, to which one's attention is to be drawn, from something ordinary, familiar, immediately accessible, into something peculiar, striking, and unexpected' (Willet 1964, p. 143). He found examples of alienation techniques in such diverse art forms as Breughel's paintings, classical Chinese theatre and German cabaret, and he borrowed freely from many sources in his attempts to create a dramatic form capable of jolting audiences into an awareness of the contradictions of capitalism.

Brecht's theatre was experimental, both in its innovatory aspects and in the sense that he would frequently rewrite scenes and speeches once he had observed audience reaction. The dramatic form which he strove to replace was the 'illusionist', slice-of-life theatre, but he recognized that his real obstacle was not this earlier theatre in itself so much as the way in which it had conditioned audience expectations and response.

Audience understanding, on the other hand, derives not merely from earlier encounters with art, but also from the integration propaganda which justifies and makes natural a particular social formation. Audiences, as Brecht saw in Zurich, were well capable of refamiliarizing and reintegrating fragmented modes of perception. In East Berlin, where one might have expected a more clearsighted understanding of Brecht's attempts at Marxist demystification, many of his plays were regarded as threats to the orthodoxies which other German writers and intellectuals had assimilated during the war years in the Soviet Union, and hence *The Days of the Commune* was banned by the Party because it was 'objectivistic' and 'defeatist' (Rühle 1969, p. 239). *Mother Courage* was attacked by Friedrich Wolf on the grounds that it failed to present a moral and political transformation of Mother Courage herself, to which Brecht could only reply, 'even if Courage learns nothing else, at least the audience, in my view, learn something by observing her (Rühle 1969, p. 236).

The demystifying power of Brecht's epic theatre hinges on this concept of an 'observing' audience, an audience, that is, which has been distanced from its normal role as participant in a sign process to the degree that it can see through the workings of its early consciousness. The dialectical nature of this mode of thinking was also clearly indicated by Shklovsky, whose comment on Tolstoy's method of 'seeing things out of their normal context' implies a vision which recognizes but is distanced from 'normal' perception. The same position, it will be recalled, was theorized by Barthes in his discussion of the *Paris-Match* illustration. Newly established post-revolutionary societies, whose integration propaganda tends to be clumsy and authoritarian, will usually react with hostility towards a literature which seems capable of producing this demystifying consciousness, as opposed to works which specifically expose the false consciousness resulting from capitalism.

This attitude, which aims to produce a concrete demystified reality rather than to generate a demystifying consciousness, was hinted at in the first recorded reference to Socialist Realism. Ivan Gronsky, Party supervisor of literature, explained in 1932 to leading Moscow literary groups: 'The basic demand that we make on the writer is: write the truth, portray truthfully our reality that is itself dialectic. Therefore the basic method of Soviet literature is the method of socialist realism' (Ermolaev 1963, p. 144). In view of this constraining aspect of Socialist Realism I cannot agree with C. Vaughan James's recent interpretation of 'the battle over formalism in the arts' as being 'from a socio-political point of view almost incidental. . . . The real battle was between conflicting theories of the nature of proletarian art, not between realism and formalism as such' (James 1973, p. 39). The real battle, it seems to me, was between conformist art and subversive art.

The official Soviet view that modernism (cubism, expressionism, surrealism, etc.) 'represented a deepening crisis in bourgeois-capitalist society and widened the gap between art and the masses' (James 1973, p. 85) may not in itself be untrue, but it has all too often served as a pretext for suppressing the sort of innovation and experimentation in literature which might induce the reader to 'see things out of their normal context'. Such views transfer the rules of artistic production from the aesthetic to the political sphere, and in doing so they transform the systematic study of aesthetic processes into a kind of prescriptive grammar.

The bullying role which this transfer grants to political leaders was well illustrated by Nikita Kruschev during his visit in 1962 to the Moscow exhibition of contemporary art. The visit seemed to have been staged in order to initiate a campaign against modernism, for Kruschev, after walking around making various derogatory comments, summed up by saying, 'Judging by these experiments, I am entitled to think that you are all pederasts, and for that you can get ten years' (Brown 1969, p. 293). Various recantations and reaffirmations of the belief in the educative function of art followed in 1963.

Realism is of course not inherently incapable of demystification. The limiting factor is produced by the addition of the modifier 'Socialist', which identifies a politically correct authorial perspective as an evaluative criterion. The 'demystifying' task of the artist, within the framework of such a definition, is not to shock readers into an awareness of contradictions within the system, but to portray only those problems and conflicts for which the system supposedly has a solution. In this sense, Socialist Realism begins to assume an uncanny resemblance to the mass culture produced in the west. A recent example of the way in which contemporary Soviet fiction glosses over conflict while purporting to discuss it is provided (unwittingly) in Felix Kuznetsov's account of Vladimir Fomenko's novel *The Memory of Soil*. The novel, which Kuznetsov uses to illustrate how 'recent Soviet literature has been probing ever deeper into the complex ethical problems of our time' (Kuznetsov 1980, p. 199), describes a small, centuries-old Cossack village which is to be demolished to make room for a giant hydro-electric project. 'The situation is laden with drama', Kuznetsov explains. 'The conflict between the social and private interests is apparent: the farmers are being asked to give up the things they cherish most for the sake of public interest, so that the nation could have more electric energy and more irrigated land' (Kuznetsov 1980, pp. 190ff.).

The role of demystification in western literature is a more complex issue, but it is equally involved with various propagandist processes. Despite bourgeois mistrust and outright censorship, literature in the west has succeeded in establishing its freedom to experiment and to shock, and this freedom has in turn manifested itself as a sustained but less than devastating attack on the social order. Daniel Bell has analysed this development in *The Cultural Contradictions of Capitalism*. He argues that 'the adversary culture has come to dominate the cultural order' (Bell 1976, p. 40), and that the transition 'from the Protestant ethic to the psychedelic bazaar' (Bell 1976, pp. 54ff.) marks the beginning of a genuine cultural revolution. In its optimistic version this thesis leads to the celebration of the 'greening of America' and to Claus Mueller's theory that the middle classes, whose educational background will lead them increasingly to see social and environmental problems as 'defects of the system rather than as temporary political aberrations' (Mueller 1973, p. 160), will emerge as a significant force for social change.

The pessimistic version is provided in Herbert Marcuse's *One-Dimensional Man*, which argues that

> The absorbent power of society depletes the artistic dimension by assimilating its antagonistic contents. In the realm of culture, the new totalitarianism manifests itself precisely in a harmonizing pluralism, where the most contradictory works and truths peacefully coexist in indifference. (Marcuse 1964, p. 61)

Bourgeois literature of the nineteenth century, even though it affirmed a power structure dominated by business and industry, was haunted by potentially antagonistic elements, by 'such disruptive characters as the artist, the prostitute, the adulteress, the great criminal and outcast, the warrior, the rebel-poet, the devil, the fool – those who don't earn a living, at least not in an orderly and normal way' (Marcuse 1964, p. 59). These characters have not been banished from literature, but have been transformed into the vamp, the national hero, the beatnik, the neurotic housewife, the gangster, the star, the charismatic tycoon and so on, and thus they become 'no longer images of another way of life but rather freaks or types of the same life, serving as an affirmation rather than negation of the established order' (Marcuse 1964, p. 59).

Marcuse's account of cultural change is in some ways the

more plausible of the two interpretations. The transformation of literature which he describes is, among other things, an explanation of one of the ways in which vertical propaganda evolves into horizontal and integration propaganda as its messages spread through society and become spontaneous. A film like *The Godfather* can thus be seen as a retroactive myth which presents gang warfare not as a threat to the established order so much as a state of violence from which the established order emerged (cf. Szanto 1978, pp. 78–84). Marcuse's thesis does not deny the existence of an adversary literature; it simply recognizes that its demystifying aspects can be absorbed or deflected by the integrating mechanisms of society.

The current schizophrenic state of potentially subversive literature seems to bear out his thesis. While on the one hand the avant-garde has retreated into an experimental play-room, on the other, writers like Günter Wallraff in West Germany have championed techniques of realistic reportage as a means of demystifying social and political structures, including the role played by the popular press in shaping and perpetuating them. Marcuse insisted that art could challenge only when it expressed a genuine 'aesthetic incompatibility with the developing society' (Marcuse 1964, p. 60), and in this sense Wallraff's method, for example of demystifying the *Bild* newspaper, seems capable of re-establishing an adversary moment able to resist – at least for a time – the integration propaganda of West German society.

Daniel Bell is no doubt right when he states that the idea of flinging 'a pot of paint in the public's face', which is what Whistler was accused of, would at the present time be a caricature of artistic rebelliousness (Bell 1976, p. 40). But this is the case only as long as we interpret the cultural changes he discusses as proof that the avant-garde has won the battle and that 'bourgeois culture has been shattered' (Bell 1976, p. 41). The freedom to be experimental, which is noisily proclaimed by the least experimental of western media every time police bulldozers break up exhibitions of modernist painting in Moscow, has in fact itself become a propaganda ploy in need of demystification. If Picasso prints are now beginning to replace flights of geese on the walls of the bourgeoisie, it is not because bourgeois culture has been shattered, but because it has dissolved itself in the knowledge that its power no longer requires a distinctive presence and clearly drawn lines of demarcation. Once the public face has vanished behind a psychedelic mask, it becomes somewhat pointless to fling a pot of paint into it.

Historically, it might seem that the bourgeoisie has retreated steadily in the face of a growing adversary culture, and that the stages of this retreat are marked by the successive handing over to the avant-garde of poetry, the novel, the drama and, to a lesser extent, the film. The battles have been colourful and heated, often involving well-publicized censorship trials, and the victorious avant-garde not surprisingly wishes to enjoy and perhaps to exaggerate its triumphs. What is easily overlooked is the fact that the bourgeoisie has not been handing over its weapons so much as discarding art forms which could no longer serve as instruments of propaganda precisely because they were becoming agents of demystification. Paradoxically, by relinquishing its hold on these forms it largely stripped them of their demystifying power. Once they had been permitted to float freely the values attached to them increasingly became elitist and intellectual. They were transformed into the toys of a liberated bohemianism which would play with them for a period while the bourgeoisie redeployed its propaganda in the art forms and media most likely to reach the masses. Today, these forms are represented chiefly by television and the press, and until advanced industrial capitalism has found equally effective vehicles for its integration propaganda it seems doubtful that the adversary culture will be permitted more than a token appearance here. It is noteworthy that the most celebrated book to have been banned recently in West Germany was Günter Wallraff's devastating exposé of the *Bild* newspaper (Wallraff 1977).

A further aspect of demystification which requires some discussion in this context is the way in which literary criticism itself has begun to emerge as an adversary activity. In part, this phenomenon might be seen as a vindication of Marcuse's cultural theories, for if literary works were themselves effectively challenging established modes of perception, there would be little need for an ancillary demystifying criticism. The schools of anti-interpretation are commonly associated with the

various structuralist and post-structuralist movements which
have flourished in France over the past twenty-five years,
especially with the work of Barthes, Althusser, Macherey,
Derrida, Kristeva and Lacan. The unifying feature is the
attempt to devise a critical method which will reveal the
ideological structures of texts, not in a 'vulgar-Marxist' reduc-
tionist way, but as linguistically constructed phenomena determined by the historicity of the discourses available to the author
as producer of meaning. Such a criticism, which the later
Barthes conceived as the necessary further development of the
demystifying strategies he had popularized in *Mythologies*,
would ultimately dismantle itself. It would become what he
called a 'semioclasty'. 'It is western discourse as such, in its
foundations, its elementary forms, that one must today attempt
to split' (Harari 1980, p. 30).

It is as yet too early to judge whether a demystifying 'semioclasty' of the kind envisaged by Barthes will emerge as a
repeatable critical method or practice. The defamiliarizing
techniques of analysis illustrated in *Mythologies* have certainly
become popular to a degree which would have been unthink-
able even twenty years ago. But this development can be seen as
coinciding with the general demythologizing tendencies which
the Vietnam War precipitated in western intellectual circles in
the late 1960s and early 1970s. Moreover, despite a shared
concern with ideological structure, post-structuralist thought
displays enormous diversity in its treatment and its definitions
of communicative processes, as is evident in the representative
examples provided in Josué Harari's excellently introduced
anthology. The very concept of an anti-interpretive method, as
Jameson has pointed out, can be understood as a demand for a
new hermeneutic model (Jameson 1981, p. 23). It should
thus be scrutinized from the perspective of a metacritical
position which would permit us to understand the way it
functions in terms other than the ones it proposes. Jameson's
The Political Unconscious, one of the most significant recent
contributions to critical theory, offers such a position in a series of
wide-ranging philosophical and critical arguments which cannot
be summarized adequately here. From the point of view of a
demystifying method or practice which might be based
on post-structuralism, two recent studies, one British and

the other West German, are worth considering in some detail. Catherine Belsey's *Critical Practice* (1980) and Peter Zima's *Textsoziologie* (1980) usefully introduce and synthesize important aspects of contemporary French thought and at the same time test its applicability within specific traditions of dealing with literary texts.

The main attraction of French thought for Belsey lies in its power to liberate the text from 'the constraints of a single and univocal reading, the text becomes available for production, plural, contradictory, capable of change' (Belsey 1980, p. 134). These constraints are identified with the main post-romantic methods of literary criticism which have dominated the formal study of literature in Britain. 'Expressive realism', a kind of fusion of Aristotelian mimesis with romantic 'overflow of powerful feelings', is seen as the main orthodoxy from which Anglo-American criticism has sought to extricate itself during this century. *New Criticism*, Northrop Frye's archetypal criticism, and the more recent work on reader response (Slatoff, Fish, Jauss, Iser), have successfully undermined aspects of this orthodoxy, but all ultimately fail because of their limited view of the way in which reality is 'discursively' created by language and because they are unable to jettison the common-sense concept of a '*humanism* based on an *empiricist-idealist* interpretation of the world' (Belsey 1980, p. 7). Such methods become insidious when they produce modes of understanding which divert readers' attention from inconsistencies which may be 'foregrounded' in texts by such authors as Brecht and Defoe. Accordingly, we need to develop methods of approaching literature which will both do justice to 'interrogative' texts (e.g. Brecht) and at the same time permit us to see through the apparent transparency of 'classic realist texts' which efface contradiction and suppress their own role in perpetuating a given social order.

Belsey seeks the elements of her new critical practice among the Ideological State Apparatuses of Althusser, the deconstructionism of Derrida, the demythifying strategies of Barthes, the textual silences of Macherey and the linguistic restructuring of Freud proposed by Lacan. The 'productive critical practice' which she would like to see replace 'consumerist criticism' sets out to seek 'not the unity of the work, but the multiplicity and diversity of its possible meanings, its incompleteness, the omissions which it displays but cannot describe, and above all its contradictions' (Belsey 1980, p. 109). Such a method would go beyond the search for a text's historical unconscious – its 'articulation of a silence' (Macherey) – for it would constantly work to produce meaning by recognizing that meanings 'circulate between text, ideology and readers whose subjectivity is discursively constructed' (Belsey 1980, p. 140). Lacan, and the later writings of Barthes, can teach us how to 'appropriate the text for the present in a more fundamental way' (Belsey 1980, p. 140). It seems to me that Belsey's most persuasive example of a demystifying critical practice is her discussion of Sherlock Holmes, which is inspired by Macherey.

In considering certain aspects of the Holmes stories, Belsey is guided particularly by Macherey's view that there can inhere within the unconscious of the text elements which contradict and throw into question the text's dominant ideology, the world view constructed from among the discourses available to the author. Her analysis contrasts the stories' apparent commitment to full scientific explanation on the one hand with their silent inability on the other to deal rationally with the sexuality of women. 'The stories begin in enigma, mystery, the impossible, and conclude with an explanation which makes it clear that logical deduction and scientific method render all mysteries accountable to reason' (Belsey 1980, p. 112). Nevertheless they 'are haunted by shadowy, mysterious and often silent women. Their silence repeatedly conceals their sexuality, investing it with a dark and magical quality which is beyond the reach of scientific knowledge' (Belsey 1980, p. 114). The classic realist text, Doyle's dominant narrative form, 'had not yet developed a way of signifying women's sexuality except in a metaphoric or symbolic mode whose presence disrupts the realist surface' (Belsey 1980, p. 115), and such elusive presentations contradict the 'project of explicitness' (Belsey 1980, p. 115) and throw into relief the 'poverty of the contemporary concept of science' (Belsey 1980, p. 115). In fact Belsey takes her argument a stage further, and should be quoted at some length:

> The classic realist text installs itself in the space between fact and illusion through the presentation of a simulated reality which is plausible but *not real*. In this lies its power as myth. It

is because fiction does not normally deal with 'politics' directly, except in the form of history or satire, that it is ostensibly innocent and therefore ideologically effective. But in its evasion of the real also lies its weakness as 'realism'. Through their transgression of their own values of explicitness and verisimilitude, the Sherlock Holmes stories contain within themselves an implicit critique of their limited nature as characteristic examples of classic realism. They thus offer the reader through the process of deconstruction a form of knowledge, not about 'life' or 'the world', but about the nature of fiction itself.

Thus, in adopting the form of classic realism, the only appropriate literary mode, positivism is compelled to display its own limitations. Offered as science, it reveals itself to a deconstructive reading as ideology at the very moment that classic realism, offered as verisimilitude, reveals itself as fiction. In claiming to make explicit and *understandable* what appears mysterious, these texts offer evidence of the tendency of positivism to push to the margins of experience whatever it cannot explain or understand. In the Sherlock Holmes stories classic realism ironically tells a truth, though not the truth about the world which is the project of classic realism. The truth the stories tell is the truth about ideology, the truth which ideology represses, its own existence as ideology itself. (Belsey 1980, p. 117)

In passages like this Belsey seems to be developing a demystifying criticism. Her commentary, by opening up new dimensions of the text's historicity, reveals some of the ways in which literature unreflectively reproduces the contradictoriness of the dominant but time-bound assumptions within a given society. Her remarks could not readily have been conceived within the framework of the Anglo-American orthodoxies she herself rejects. On the other hand, these antecedents are not really relevant to Belsey's work as alternative methods of interpretation, for Belsey is not *merely* borrowing from recent French thought in order to reform the study of literature in Britain; she is implicitly urging that traditional literary criticism should be transformed into a kind of dialectical sociology of the (literary) text, and this aim should be set within a much broader framework of theory and critical practice. Such a framework is attempted by Peter V. Zima.

Zima's *Textsoziologie: Eine kritische Einführung* clarifies at the very outset its own epistemological presuppositions. Quoting with approval Althusser's remark that the whole class struggle can sometimes be reduced to a clash between words, Zima goes on to develop the idea that neither science nor literature can claim to possess value-free, neutral discourses:

> This recognition is something new in the field of literary sociology. While the empirical methods, obeying the principle of the division of labour, have handed over the question of text *structure* to philology and literary criticism, Marxists have accustomed themselves to talking about literature not as if it were a *text*, a verbal system of signs, but purely as 'art'. (Zima 1980, p. 1)

Empirical literary sociologists in the Weber tradition (Silbermann, Fügen, Escarpit, Rosengren, etc.) not only mistakenly confuse traditional academic objectivity with value-free discourse; by refraining from discussing the aesthetic dimension of literature they also sustain the view that the essence of art is itself somehow autonomous and isolated from social or group interests. A properly constituted sociology of texts would be a kind of discourse criticism, 'a critical science, which has as its object the structure of the text' (Zima 1980, p. 21). As such it would turn not to empirical sociology but to the dialectical literary sociologists such as Lukács, Althusser, Goldmann and Adorno. Of these, Lukács and Goldmann, although providing many valuable insights, are theoretically inadequate in that they fail to make a complete break with Hegel's influence on the way in which art was seen as reflecting an independent 'totality'. Althusser, Macherey and, above all, Adorno have liberated the text from this impasse by drawing attention to the contradictions expressed and implied by it. In the process, they have also drawn attention to the historicity of language itself, and to the view that ideology, far from being an independent entity expressed through language, is in fact linguistically constructed.

A sociology of the text must go beyond these beginnings, Zima argues, for it must be able to show precisely how 'ideologemes' manifest themselves in narrative, semantic and phonetic structures:

> A text sociology must be capable of explaining the significance of syntactic, narrative, and semantic events within the fictive mode of writing: at the same time, if it wishes to bridge the gap between the text and its context, it must be able to represent social structures as linguistic. (Zima 1980, p. 52)

In order to find useful models for such an undertaking, Zima borrows from the structural semantics of Greimas, the semiology of Mukařovský, and especially from the work of Bakhtin and his co-workers in Leningrad. The main ideas lead to the concept of a 'sociolect', comprising lexicon, code and discursive structures. Each of the discursive structures can be seen as a special realization of the sociolect (a 'mise en discours' in the terms of Greimas). The code, within Zima's terms, is strictly the 'repertory of discursive deep structures' of a given sociolect (Zima 1980, p. 75).

Despite such a formidable arsenal of analytic instruments and theoretical models, Zima's fragmentary and hurried application of his method to a number of literary texts (by Musil, Proust, Kafka and Hesse) is rather disappointing. His discussion of Musil's *Der Mann ohne Eigenschaften* is impressive in its treatment of the ironic play on different discourses, and his comments on Kafka, especially on the relationship of his ambivalent semantic world to the 'disintegration of narrative syntax' (Zima 1980, p. 148), are enlightening. There is little here, however, that could not conceivably have been produced by the traditional techniques of close reading informed by a knowledge of cultural history. Zima is not unaware of this, for in his final chapter he distances himself from a dogmatic methodological position in order to argue that the genre of the essay, with its capacity for associative thinking and self-reflection, should become the dominant means of expressing insights into literary-sociological phenomena.

Interestingly, the contributions of both Belsey and Zima can be seen as extensions of their respective national traditions as well as the beginning of a new international criticism. In her determination to question radically the notion of an accepted canon of 'great' works of literature, the 'great tradition' proposed by F. R. Leavis and others, Belsey has to some extent turned its techniques against texts such a canon would itself have excluded. Her own critical practice is marked by a virtuosity and an elegance which are not easily reproducible, and it can be located only partially within the terms of the French theories she cites. The illuminating aspects of her technique, like those of the traditional methods she seeks to replace, illuminate precisely because they are concerned with hitherto inadequately explored dimensions of literary experience. In West Germany, where there has been a steady stream of practical anti-criticism from the 1960s to the present, Zima responds to the German tradition which demands a full scientific and theoretical explanation of observable phenomena. His discourse-splitting theorems are as dazzling within his literary tradition as is Belsey's practical criticism within hers. Both books are relevant to the study of sociological propaganda, but neither has managed to develop a systematic and teachable method of discourse-splitting as demystification. Taken together, however, both studies provide a useful practical and theoretical foundation upon which further approaches to a broader range of materials might be developed.

8
Fiction
and reality

Steve Neale has recently attempted to specify the theoretical bases of propaganda in relation to the cinema. His main aim is to differentiate films into which a specific ideology has been inscribed in a non-propagandist manner from films made within the context of a 'specific, politically motivated, ideological intervention by the Nazi state' (Neale 1977, p. 9). His two poles of investigation are the populist films made in Hollywood during the 1930s and two anti-semitic films released in Germany in 1940, *Jud Süß* and *Der ewige Jude*. Neale distances himself from 'liberal humanist' definitions of propaganda, in which all ideologies are ideological except one's own, and develops a method which moves analytically between the structural features of the films and describable aspects of audience reception. Within the classificatory framework produced by this method, the Hollywood populist films are neither structured as propaganda, nor was there any possibility of Hollywood's films 'functioning as propaganda, at least within the United States itself' (Neale 1977, p. 39). On the other hand, the documentary *Der ewige Jude* is held to be propagandist, mainly because it signifies discourses and practices in such a way 'as to mark them as existing outside and beyond it [i.e., the film]. It is this position that I would maintain as the fundamental mark of a propagandist text' (Neale 1977, p. 31). *Jud Süß*, because of its classical realist mode of address, cannot be regarded as propagandist in a structural sense (Neale 1977, p. 25), but it is considered to have served a 'propagandist function' deriving from the nature of its historical reception. The film was widely used, by Himmler and others, as a means of forestalling and nullifying any possible sympathy for the victims of Nazi 're-settlement'. The film is none the less a 'classical fictional text' (Neale 1977, p. 29), and as such it cannot be formally viewed as propaganda.

Neale's contribution is a useful and important attempt to establish a conceptual space for propaganda within the metacritical framework presupposed by much recent British criticism concerned with ideology in literature and art. Outside this framework his specification becomes somewhat less convincing, both because of the narrow scope of his definition of propaganda and on account of the way he theorizes fictivity as opposed to documentariness. The narrowness of definition is of course to some extent a question of terminology. *Der ewige Jude*, the only film considered by Neale to possess the 'fundamental mark of a propagandist text', would be classified within the terms I have proposed as a variant form of a much more broadly defined phenomenon, namely as vertical, political, agitation propaganda specifically designed by the Nazis as a means of subverting and rearranging the structure of beliefs and moral principles commonly regarded as 'conscience'. Populist films such as *Ruggles of Red Gap* and *Mr Deeds Goes to Washington* would similarly be defined as examples of integration propaganda reaffirming collective beliefs in the classlessness of American society, national regeneration from the grass roots led by Abraham Lincoln figures and so on. Many of these early Hollywood films, in an interesting historical twist, portrayed the British as a nation in a manner reminiscent of the way in which British literature of the post-industrial revolution period had represented the aristocracy. If we deny these films even the possibility of 'functioning as propaganda' it becomes difficult to explain adequately the transition which took place in the war years, when Hollywood consciously set about creating a more favourable and democratic image of the English upper classes in such films as *Mrs Miniver* and *The White Cliffs of Dover* (Kracauer 1957, p. 268).

The more problematic issue raised by Neale, and one which

leads to a highly controversial question in the history of literary theory, is the distinction he makes between the fictional *Jud Süß* and the documentary *Der ewige Jude*. Neal argues that *Jud Süß* was able to *function* as propaganda, *despite* its fictional structure, because of the apparatuses of its 'production, distribution and consumption' (Neale 1977, p. 34). Superficially, this position might be understood as a modification of the 'strong' version of fictionality, according to which statements in a literary text can only refer to a 'world of fiction', can only 'seem' to convey information, and can never be 'logical propositions' (Wellek and Warren 1956, pp. 25–6).

But Neale does not exactly modify this view; he challenges it as a theory by testing it against his empirical observation of a historical sign process. The semiosis he analyses involved Goebbels, who personally supervised the production of *Jud Süß*; the structure of the film itself, which like *Der ewige Jude* juxtaposed images in order to suggest that the 'civilized' Jew was a mask concealing the true features and nature of the 'real' Jew; and finally the specific audiences, including SS groups and 'Aryan' residents of the Eastern Territories, to whom the film was shown as a prelude to the 'final solution of the Jewish question'. Some structural features of the film, which Neale attributes to Nazi propaganda and interprets according to his reconstruction of historical reception, are interpretants which function communicatively in much the same way as the interpretants of *Der ewige Jude*.

Once we have granted these interpretants a specific historicity within a sign process the distinction between fictional texts and documentary texts begins to lose its meaning, for the relevant relation is not that which obtains between a text and the way it marks its own referentiality, but rather the relation between the designata of a text and the modes of perception accompanying a particular historical act of reception. This clearly does not mean that the immediate historical reception of a text can co-determine its meaning for all time, but it does suggest that fictionality is a relative historical category which should be explained in terms of reception rather than textual structure. A text may seem able to signal fictionality, but it achieves this only when its receivers are subject to a set of shared conventions.

One of the tasks of propaganda is to disrupt these conventions, e.g. to strengthen them in order to diminish the social or political import of a literary text, or to break them down to the point where a text can be regarded as expressing 'logical propositions'. In order to investigate literature as propaganda we have to give up traditional methods of theorizing fictionality and situational contexts. For propaganda, in all its forms, assumes both its receivers and its situational contexts to be real historical entities.

When we look back today at various Nazi propaganda films, it may seem possible to fix them at different points on a spectrum ranging from fictional to documentary. *Frederick the Great* would be at one end, *Der ewige Jude* at the other and *Jud Süß* somewhere in between. From the point of view of reception in the Third Reich, however, this type of structural differentiation is insignificant, for all three films functioned similarly in the way they manipulated interpretants. Of the three, it is likely that *Frederick the Great* might at some point be received as fictional, because the interpretants which identified Frederick with Hitler derived from intention and reception rather than from textual structure. In other words, the designata of *Frederick the Great* did not further denote within the structure of the film a set of historical correspondences. Rather the film-makers anticipated that German audiences at the time would furnish the desired references and understand the film as a 'logical proposition', or transparent pointer. *Frederick the Great* can thus be seen as an example of Nazi integration propaganda, which both utilized and reinforced the schemes of interpretation which National Socialism had imposed on history, or to be more precise, on the earlier interpretative schemes which had been applied to German history.

The difference between *Frederick the Great* and *Jud Süß* does not derive from degrees of fictionality so much as from the distinction which can be made between integration and agitation within a given historical situation. From various speeches and secret documents we know that even in 1940 the Nazi leaders were concerned that a residual 'softness' in German society might impede their plans to destroy Europe's Jews. The death camps, in contrast to the concentration camps, were never used as an instrument of psychological terror against the civilian population of Germany, and to a large extent their existence, or at least the purpose of their existence, was kept secret. The agitational function of films like *Jud Süß* and *Der ewige Jude* was to subvert the moral resistance of those groups who for various reasons might become aware of the true meaning of the 'final solution'. Thus these two films, unlike *Frederick the Great*, were not co-operating with reception interpretants, but were acting to 'cut down the intervening sign processes of which the individual is capable' (Morris 1971, p. 296). They were aiming to produce new reception interpretants which would redefine the relation between the individual and 'reality'.

The films work in a complementary and mutually reinforcing manner to achieve this effect, for when *Der ewige Jude* documents the 'facts' about Jews it becomes the context of 'reality' within which the deeper truth of the 'fictional' *Jud Süß* can be perceived. The fictional *Jud Süß*, on the other hand, becomes the context of universal symbolic truth within which the documentary becomes valid and timeless. Further insight into the way in which fiction becomes state-approved reality could be gained from a detailed comparative analysis of *Jud Süß* and the novel by Lion Feuchtwanger on which it was ostensibly based. I shall not attempt such a comparison here, but it should be pointed out that the novel, which appeared in 1925, was banned by the Nazis in 1933. One of the secondary functions of the film was no doubt to erase the memory of Feuchtwanger's implication of a European Jewry surviving persecution.

The 'strong' version of fictionality, with which Steve Neale's structuralist understanding of fictional classic realism should not be confused, is now becoming something of an historical curiosity. It deserves some discussion, however, both as an illustration of how 'flat earth' thinking can come to dominate twentieth-century literary theory, and as a striking example of criticism functioning as propaganda. It is not a theory in any strict sense, but rather a declaration concerning the mode of existence of art, from which principles for the correct method of understanding literature can supposedly be derived. Wayne Booth has listed the main slogans of the movement as follows:

The defining characteristic of art is that it does not argue, is not didactic. 'Poetry makes nothing happen.' 'A poem should

not mean but be.' 'There are no beliefs in poetry, only
pseudo-beliefs.' 'The difference between a novel and a tract is
that a novel offers no propositions that ask to be tested for
their truth value.' 'The *poetic* is a domain entirely different
from the domains of discursive speculation or of practical
decision and action.' Thus to ask what a novel, play, poem,
symphony, or painting proves, to ask what good reasons any
genuine work of art gives for any change of mind, is to commit
an absurd confusion of categories. (Booth 1974, p. 165)

The problem with all this, Booth continues, is that it flies in the
face of experience. He explains that he became an active
member of the NAACP (National Association for the Advancement of Colored People) not by listening to discursive arguments, but 'by reading works like *Uncle Tom's Cabin* and Lillian
Smith's *Strange Fruit,* and by hearing Billie Holiday sing the
song of the same name . . . by the age of 20 my opinions and
emotions were very largely a product – as I know they must be
still – of the art I had encountered' (Booth 1974, p. 166).

How, then, did such theories, which are contradicted by
personal experience and empirical observation, manage to
establish themselves as one of the cornerstones of New Criticism? The defensive explanation is that such a view serves to
protect art from censorship. This is largely wishful thinking, for
censorship by definition always proceeds from the empirical
assumptions advanced on its behalf by Plato more than 2000
years ago: art can corrupt; it can frighten children and disrupt
authority; writers can be guilty of 'the most serious mis-
statements about human life' (Plato 1951, p. 78). Philip Sidney's famous words, according to which the poet 'nothing
affirmeth, and therefore never lieth', have never been taken
seriously by the forces of censorship. The notorious 1966 Moscow trial against Andrey Sinyavsky and Yuli Daniel, who had
been accused of Anti-Soviet propaganda, was dominated by a
prosecution which revolved constantly around the question:
'Why did you write works that could be interpreted as Anti-
Soviet?' (Labedz and Hayward 1967, p. 174). Defence witnesses
who tried to put forward fictionality theories were ridiculed or
interrupted in mid-sentence by a judge who attached sinister
significance even to the fact that the cover of one of the books

being investigated was two-thirds black and 'only one-third red' (Labedz and Hayward 1967, p. 105).

In the United States, where fictionality assumed its most dogmatic and doctrinaire forms in the post-war years, ideas about the self-contained world of art were none the less brushed aside in favour of an empirical approach by the presidential commission on pornography whose report was published in 1970. No literary or art experts had been appointed to the commission, but the final report contains numerous references to the relationship between society and literature (Levin 1973, p. 113). The panel did question police chiefs, 58 per cent of whom linked pornography with juvenile crime (Levin 1973, p. 116), and they derived empirical data from the use of a 'phallo-plethysmograph' which supposedly correlated sexual arousal to erotic literature (Levin 1973, p. 117). Despite all this, the report did not tell the politicians what they wanted to hear, and it was condemned in the Senate by a vote of 60 to 5 (Levin 1973, p. 112).

In recent years, the notion that fictionality constitutes a defence against censorship has been challenged by the view which sees such theories as being themselves propagandistic. By diverting the reader's attention into a realm of auto-referentiality and aestheticism, they obscure the relationship between art and life, and in effect function as a kind of secondary censorship controlling reception rather than production. In America, where these theories became a basic tenet of New Criticism, and where they still linger on in the current debate about literature and speech-act theory (Juhl 1980, pp. 153–95), the reaction against them was especially heated. In 1970 Bruce Franklin described New Criticism as a 'conscious counterattack on rising proletarian culture', and stated:

> In the present era, formalism is the use of aestheticism to blind us to social and moral reality. It is the expression of the mentality of Mussolini's son, who was thrilled by the beauty of the bursting bombs he dropped on the Ethiopian villages. (Franklin 1972, p. 113)

Franklin's identification of these views with 'formalism' should not be taken as an expression of Zhdanovism, but rather as recognition of the fact that some of the influential theorists of

New Criticism had popularized and overstated certain aspects of Russian Formalist thought. Russian Formalism, when detached from the social implications of defamiliarization discussed earlier, can appear to degenerate into a one-sided 'art for art's sake' approach. Victor Shklovsky, for example, argued in 1923 against identifying revolutionary art with actual social revolution: 'Art was always apart from life and its colour never reflected the colour of the flag that waved over the fortress of the city' (Wellek 1976, p. 40). Roman Jakobson and René Wellek introduced these ideas into the main current of American literary criticism, and Jakobson particularly, no doubt keenly aware of the way Soviet aesthetics had crushed the Formalist movement to which he had belonged, tended to exaggerate the effects of denying the auto-referential character of art. The confusion between life and art, he suggested, turns us 'into a medieval audience which wants to beat up the actor who played Judas' (Wellek 1976, p. 40; cf. Hawkes 1977, p. 86).

These formalist theories could not have exerted such a potent influence, however, had they not coincided with a general social categorization of art which had been developing in the bourgeois capitalist countries. The East German theorist Robert Weimann, in his penetrating critique of the origins and nature of New Criticism, traces the movement back to 'Victorian aestheticism', to a general view of culture which identified the enjoyment of literature with cosy armchairs in comfortable domestic libraries. This view is exemplified in such books as W. H. Hudson's *A Quiet Corner in a Library* (1915), prefaced by a poem containing the stanzas:

> The night has fallen early,
> With a welter of wind and rain;
> 'Tis a dismal scene that meets my gaze
> Through the blurred window-pane.
>
> So I draw the curtains quickly,
> And shut it away from sight,
> And turn to my little book-lined world
> Of love, and warmth, and light. (Weimann 1974, p. 25)

New Criticism thus becomes the specific literary-critical manifestation of a general tendency to 'shut it away from sight'; to seek shelter from reality in a world of abstractions and eternal truths. Joan Rockwell has wittily mocked the blinkered vision which such tendencies produce:

> When academics are born, a good fairy at the christening promises them that when they grow up they will be able to read and understand books. Hardly has she finished speaking, however, when a bad fairy interrupts to say, with a threatening gesture, 'But you must never, never look out of the window'. (Rockwell 1974, p. vii)

It might be assumed that literary techniques of realism, by making explicit the correspondence between literary sign and social reality, are available as a permanent means of overcoming the modes of perception which deny art its relationship to life. Scores of such texts have been listed and discussed by David Craig and Michael Egan in their recent book *Extreme Situations* (1979), which deals with the sort of twentieth-century literature that can be seen as 'a form of bulletin from the front lines of history'. The authors point out that many of the writers they discuss, precisely because they were the most telling witnesses, were also the most likely to be 'ignored, forgotten or silenced' (Craig and Egan 1979, p. 11). This is true, but one must also add that realism, like fictionality, is a fluctuating category of reception. Texts must continuously develop new expressive forms in order to be received as 'real'. This relativity becomes apparent when we consider texts which have employed modern realistic techniques in order to shock readers into a moral condemnation of war. When these techniques were first used, notably by Henri Barbusse in his novel *Under Fire* (1917), they undoubtedly functioned in a demystifying way. Wilfred Owen, during the same war, used to carry in his pocket a collection of battle-field photographs which he would silently hand to the armchair warriors he encountered in England between his periods on the Front (Gardner 1964, p. xx). Barbusse's 'befouled faces and tattered flesh' (Barbusse 1917, p. 338) and Owen's photographs may have been powerful images of defamiliarization sixty-five years ago, but today they would be submerged by the bulletins 'from the front lines of history' which the media dish up with breakfast.

The struggle for a new realism, and the recognition that

realism must constantly anticipate and adapt itself to reception strategies, has been especially evident during recent years in West Germany. Many writers, including Günter Grass, Heinrich Böll, Hans Magnus Enzensberger, Rolf Hochhuth and Peter Weiss, disturbed by West Germany's apparent ability to live peacefully with the memory of the Third Reich, have attempted to develop techniques capable of demystifying both the past and contemporary attitudes towards it. Traditional realist methods, employed by Carl Zuckmayer in *The Devil's General* (1946) and Ernst Wiechert in the autobiographical account of his imprisonment in Buchenwald (*Der Totenwald*, 1946), not only failed to demystify but, by demonizing the Third Reich (Zuckmayer), or presenting it as part of a 'symphony of death' (Wiechert), contributed to the formation of the very interpretants which prevented a clearsighted confrontation with the horrors of Nazi Germany. Even Hochhuth's play *The Deputy* (1963), despite its brilliant demystification of language as a protection against reality, perpetuated the myth of a demonic Third Reich, both by presenting the Doctor as a Mephistophelean figure and by depicting Auschwitz in Act Five as a kind of modern Hades.

Hochhuth's drama none the less marks an important stage in the movement towards documentary realism which culminated in Peter Weiss's drama *The Investigation* (1966), based on the court record of the Frankfurt Auschwitz trial of 1964–5. Weiss's use of documentary techniques, which stands in sharp contrast to the experimental theatre of his earlier *Marat/Sade* (1964), reflects his growing conviction that a contemporary literature of commitment must move away from a 'faded' literary tradition and seek its inspiration in 'the most intimate personal statements . . . diaries . . . reports from prisons' (Rischbieter 1967, pp. 23–4). Thus Weiss's documentary plays, beginning with *The Investigation*, can be seen as a conscious rejection both of the avant-garde and of the view which insists that: 'To bring anything really to life in literature we can't be lifelike: we have to be literature-like' (Frye 1964, p. 91).

Literary protest against the Vietnam war was slow to manifest itself in West Germany, and in fact the first important voice to be heard was that of Erich Fried, an Austrian writer who has lived in England since before the Second World War. The forty-one poems contained in his *und Vietnam und* (1966, Berlin) none the less mark an important development for, as Ulla Hahn has pointed out (Hahn 1978, pp. 36ff.), they not only address themselves directly and unambiguously to contemporary events; they also, and more significantly, establish the imaginative writer as an interpreter and unmasker of the fabric of documentary reality created by the media.

Insofar as this new challenge was taken up through the medium of poetry, Günter Grass was probably right in speaking disparagingly of the 'wooden sword and missing tooth' of the protest song (Hahn 1978, p. 38). An adversary interpretation of reality is impotent as long as it functions merely as an eloquent authentication of the views and feelings of a very small minority who respond to its expressive forms. Unlike Grass, some other authors were not content to separate their writing from political and social action, and they set themselves the task of creating literary forms capable of reaching and influencing the recipients of the partial yet realistic documentary images and interpretations of reality put out by the media. Günter Wallraff, the leading figure to emerge from this movement, has argued that not 'literature as art' but only 'literature as reality' is capable of penetrating a politicized consciousness and of producing social change (Wallraff 1973, p. 265). His three books on the *Bild* newspaper, together with his collection of *Reportagen* on various aspects of contemporary German political, military and industrial attitudes, expose strikingly a number of basic contradictions in German society and the role of the popular press in concealing them. His technique of realism, which explicitly rejects the notion that contemporary writing can persuade through imaginative invention and intensity of image, derives from his ability to present events and experiences before they have been processed by the consciousness industry. The defamiliarizing effect of these matter-of-fact chronicles results partly from the fact that, in his search for authentic encounters with officialdom, information policies, etc., Wallraff frequently assumes a social role or identity other than his own, and thus he becomes both participant in and observer of a communicative system. In his piece on napalm (Wallraff 1976, pp. 333–47) he posed as a catholic chemist, whose research had yielded a new and cheap way of synthesizing the main constituent of napalm, and who was seeking moral advice on whether he should accept massive orders from the American military during the Vietnam war. An invention, in two senses, thus becomes the means of entry into a factually presented and chilling series of ethical discussions with identified German priests and professors of moral theology.

Wallraff's methods will no doubt in time be co-opted and debased by the very discourses which he demystifiés. But at present it seems to me that his work constitutes the most effective example of writing as anti-propaganda. His reports, unlike, say, the demystifying TV plays of Jim Allen (*Days of Hope*, *The Spongers*, *United Kingdom*) have been structured so as to forestall the process whereby a discussion of poetic truth can suppress the question of historical truth.

9

Demystifying the witch hunt (*Arthur Miller*)

In this final section I propose to consider in some detail Arthur Miller's play *The Crucible*. My aim is not to interpret the play in any traditional sense, but to investigate the historical processes of communication with which, in its day, it was involved and which it attempted to challenge. Although critics have frequently attached 'propaganda value' to *The Crucible*, and have in fact speculated on how this value might have been enhanced with different characterization (Weales 1977, p. 343), I have proceeded from the assumption that the play should properly be regarded not as propagandist but as attempted demystification of propaganda.

In the early 1950s, when *The Crucible* was conceived, the processes of American politics were in danger of being subverted by a noisy campaign of agitation propaganda which, historically, could be seen as an attempt to exploit a general susceptibility to agitation which tends to linger on after national crises such as war. Cate Haste has documented a similar period in British history, when after the end of the First World War the Northcliffe press and various politicians successfully utilized the alarmist hysteria which had been fostered by four-and-a-half years of scurrilous anti-German propaganda (Haste 1977, pp. 179ff.).

Allied propaganda in the Second World War, while not giving up the 'blond beast' and 'yellow peril' strategies, took into greater account the need to explain what people were fighting for and what institutions they were defending. In Britain this took the form of promises and legislation designed to promote social reform, of which the 1944 Education Act is an example. In the United States there was a stronger tendency to resort to abstractions and emotive appeals to 'democracy', the 'American way of life', etc., all of which worked to produce a powerful but rather vague consciousness of forces threatening to destroy American values. Even the quantitative semanticists employed on war communications research and propaganda detection were unable to distance themselves from this sort of thinking. 'In periods of crisis', one of them argued, 'it is peculiarly necessary to identify enemies of democracy' (Lasswell *et al.* 1965, p. 175); and, 'The balance of what we read, see and hear needs to be strongly tilted on the side of democracy. . . . We cannot afford to be complacent in the presence of news and comment that undermine our fundamental faith and practice' (Lasswell *et al.* 1965, p. 176).

Such phrases as 'enemies of democracy' and 'fundamental faith and practice' may be informative in certain contexts, but they also lend themselves to valuative and incitive usages; they provide opportunities for speakers to change 'the denotation of certain common terms while continuing to use the existing appraisive and prescriptive features of their signification' (Morris 1971, p. 226). Members of the House Un-American Activities Committee exploited these incitive possibilities with effective ruthlessness; their hearings and accusations made credible the concept of the 'enemy within', and they plunged American society into the greatest institutionalized witch hunt in US history.

The Crucible, in exploring and exposing the interpretants of such processes, and in investigating the historical and moral conditions which make them effective, is essentially a piece of anti-propaganda. When the play appeared Miller was accused of having falsified the past and the present, and three years later he himself was summoned to appear before the House Committee (Rovere 1962, pp. 276ff.). His words to the committee – 'I will protect my sense of myself' – are an uneasy reminder of the role he had created for John Proctor, the contemporary relevance of which had been denied by many reviewers.

When Miller's *Collected Plays* appeared in 1957, the author wrote an Introduction which provides numerous insights into his views concerning the relationship of dramatic art to social reality, and into his concept of the theatre's ultimate moral function. Discussing drama as a reflection of contemporary ideas, beliefs and feelings, he remarked:

These plays, in one sense, are my response to what was 'in the air', and they are one man's way of saying to his fellow men, 'This is what you see every day, or think or feel; now I will show you what you really know but have not had the time, or the disinterestedness, or the insight, or the information to understand consciously'. Each of these plays, in varying degrees, was begun in the belief that it was unveiling a truth already known but unrecognized as such. My concept of the audience is of a public each member of which is carrying about with him what he thinks is an anxiety, or a hope, or a preoccupation which is his alone and isolates him from mankind; and in this respect at least the function of a play is to reveal him to himself so that he may touch others by virtue of the revelation of his mutuality with them. If only for this reason I regard the theater as a serious business, one that makes or should make man more human, which is to say, less alone. (Miller 1957, p. 11)

In the later discussion of *The Crucible* in the same Introduction, Miller returns to these ideas and develops them more specifically. Technical and theatrical considerations, he wrote, were a

preparation for what turned out to be *The Crucible*, but 'what was in the air' provided the actual locus of the tale. If the reception of all *All My Sons* and *Death of a Salesman* had made the world a friendly place for me, events of the early fifties quickly turned that warmth into an illusion. (Miller 1957, p. 39)

The specific event of the early 1950s referred to by Miller was the frenzy of anti-communist activity generally but somewhat misleadingly known as 'McCarthyism'. If *The Crucible* is a dramatic symbol for the 'witch-hunting' activities of Joseph McCarthy and his followers, however, Miller makes it clear that he considers the activities themselves to possess a significance which far transcends even the considerable importance attached to them by some contemporary observers. In a curious way, in fact, Miller had conceived of McCarthy as a key to the understanding of the historical Salem witch trials before he applied himself to the task of portraying the trials so as to illuminate issues of his own times. The Salem witch hunt, which he had known of for many years, had always remained 'an inexplicable darkness' until he was able to look into it 'with the contemporary situation at my back, particularly the mystery of handing over conscience' (Miller 1957, p. 41). Before examining more closely Miller's views on the broad historical and moral relevance of these events, it might be instructive to sketch briefly those aspects of McCarthyism which were, so to speak, 'in the air' at the time, and which can contribute to our deeper understanding of *The Crucible* within the terms which Miller himself considered to be important.

Joseph R. McCarthy (1908–57), Republican Senator from Wisconsin, became nationally known in the early part of 1950 following a speech delivered to the Republican Women's Club of Wheeling, West Virginia. The speech, which was simply one expression of a general Republican attempt to exploit popular fears of communism and subversion, drew attention to itself mainly because of the apparently detailed information which McCarthy claimed to possess. At one point, for example, he brandished a piece of paper and shouted,

I have here in my hand a list of 205 – a list of names that were made known to the Secretary of State as being members of the Communist Party and who nevertheless are still working and shaping policy in the State Department. (Griffith 1970, p. 49)

McCarthy's allegations, given wide press coverage the following day, seemed to confirm an ever-widening belief in the United States that certain legal and political events could be explained only in terms of conspiracy. The conviction of Alger Hiss in America on charges of perjury in connection with espionage, the first report of a nuclear explosion in the Soviet

Union, the arrest and confession of the British physicist and spy
Klaus Fuchs and the defeat of Chiang Kai-shek's Nationalist
armies in China; all these events were interpreted by some
politicians and certain elements of the mass media – especially
the newspapers in the Hearst and Scripps-Howard chains – as
irrefutable evidence of the Great Conspiracy. The special logic
required in order to make the sign fit the interpretation, rather
than vice-versa, is well illustrated in a further speech which
McCarthy delivered in June 1951. 'How can we account for our
present situation', he asked,

> *unless* we believe that men high in this government are
> concerting to deliver us to disaster? This *must be* the product of
> a great conspiracy. . . . A conspiracy of infamy so black that,
> when it is finally exposed, its principals shall be forever
> deserving of the maledictions of all honest men. (Hofstadter
> 1966, p. 7)

Such rhetoric met with widespread acceptance and led to a
mood of repression and intimidation. McCarthy's accusations
became more extravagant as support for his claims grew,
culminating in January 1954 when a Gallup Poll revealed that
the Senator enjoyed a popularity rating of 50 per cent (Griffith
1970, p. 263). His nationally televised investigation of the Army,
together with a series of unrestrained attacks on the political
conduct of President Eisenhower, led finally in December
1954 to a Senate Resolution which 'condemned' McCarthy for
conduct 'unbecoming a Member of the United States Senate'.

Arthur Miller was struck particularly by the social trans-
formations precipitated by the rise of McCarthyism, an event
which he found less 'weird and mysterious' than the

> fact that a political, objective, knowledgeable campaign from
> the far Right was capable of creating not only a terror, but a
> new subjective reality. . . . I saw forming a kind of interior
> mechanism of confession and forgiveness of sins which until
> now had not been rightly categorized as sins. New sins were
> being created monthly. . . . Above all, above all horrors, I saw
> accepted the notion that conscience was no longer a private
> matter but one of state administration. I saw men handing

conscience to other men and thanking other men for the opportunity of doing so. (Miller 1957, pp. 39–40)

That Miller should have found counterparts to such phenomena in history is not in itself surprising, for McCarthyism in a wider context can be recognized as an extreme manifestation of beliefs and attitudes with firmly established precedents in American society. Robert Griffith, who cites such precursors to the early 1950s as the Alien and Sedition acts, immigration restriction, anti-syndicalist laws and a disposition to deny freedom of speech, press and assembly to American communists, regards the anti-communist movement as having 'informed and in some cases dominated American politics for more than fifty years' (Griffith 1970, p. 31). In a still broader social sense it is possible to see McCarthyism not merely as an extreme expression of recurrent anti-radical sentiment, but as a manifestation of what Richard Hofstadter has described as the 'paranoid style' in American politics. This concept, which of course is by no means confined to American society, provides an illuminating framework for understanding the events in seventeenth-century Salem depicted in *The Crucible*, the various political issues 'in the air' in the early 1950s, and at the same time Miller's artistic insights into the interrelatedness of the two sets of occurrences.

The paranoid style in politics, as defined by Hofstadter, differs from clinical paranoia in one crucial way:

Although they both tend to be overheated, oversuspicious, overaggressive, grandiose, and apocalyptic in expression, the clinical paranoid sees the hostile and conspiratorial world in which he feels himself to be living as directed specifically *against him*; whereas the spokesman of the paranoid style finds it directed against a nation, a culture, a way of life whose fate affects not himself alone but millions of others. . . . His sense that his political passions are unselfish and patriotic, in fact, goes far to intensify his feeling of righteousness and his moral indignation. (Hofstadter 1966, p. 4)

The paranoid style, as Hofstadter points out and documents, is deeply rooted in the political history of the United States. The Bavarian Illuminati, Catholics, Freemasons and various other groups have been seen at different times as vast and sinister conspiracies dedicated to the overthrow of established moral and social order. In more recent years such institutions as the United Nations and Marshall Aid have been regarded as part of an international communist conspiracy, while even the fluoridation of drinking water has been viewed by certain groups as 'an attempt to advance socialism under the guise of public health or to rot out the brains of the community by introducing chemicals in the water supply in order to make people more vulnerable to socialist or communist schemes' (Hofstadter 1966, p. 6). The most striking contemporary exponents of such views have no doubt been Robert H. Welch and his followers in the John Birch Society, who a few years ago proclaimed that 'Communist influences are now in almost complete control of our Federal Government' (Hofstadter 1966, p. 27), a statement which is hardly unexpected when taken together with Welch's view of Eisenhower as a 'dedicated, conscious agent of the Communist conspiracy' (Hofstadter 1966, p. 28).

The paranoid disposition, Hofstadter concludes, is likely to become especially prominent in periods of social conflict in which ultimate values are thrown into question; fears and hatreds, rather than 'negotiable interests' (Hofstadter 1966, p. 39), are then brought into political action. The paranoid, because of his developing resistance to any real historical awareness, is in a sense a double sufferer, 'since he is afflicted not only by the real world, with the rest of us, but by his fantasies as well' (Hofstadter 1966, p. 40).

There are periods in history when these fantasies threaten to become the dominant interpretants of a given society. This is surely what Arthur Miller found so disconcerting when he commented on the new 'subjective reality' which appeared on the American scene together with the rise of McCarthyism, and which led him to state, 'It was as though the whole country had been born anew, without a memory even of certain elemental decencies which a year or two earlier no one would have imagined could be altered, let alone forgotten' (Miller 1957, p. 39). Elizabeth and John Proctor, in *The Crucible*, represent the point of view of those who find themselves plunged into a world in which paranoid fantasy is establishing itself as the official

scheme of interpretation. Early in the play, when they first hear
of the arrests and the setting up of a court in Salem, they believe
that the madness can be brought to a swift end by a few words of
explanation and common sense:

> ELIZABETH: The Deputy Governor promise hangin' if they'll
> not confess, John. The town's gone wild, I think. She speak of
> Abigail, and I thought she were a saint, to hear her. Abigail
> brings the other girls into the court, and where she walks the
> crowd will part like the sea for Israel. And folks are brought
> before them, and if they scream and howl and fall to the floor –
> the person's clapped in the jail for bewitchin' them.
>
> PROCTOR, *wide-eyed*: Oh, it is a black mischief.
>
> ELIZABETH: I think you must go to Salem, John. *He turns to her.*
> I think so. You must tell them it is a fraud. (Miller 1957,
> p. 263)

Events in Salem, however, are no longer to be interpreted
according to the facts; the facts rather must be fitted into an
all-embracing theory of conspiracy on behalf of the Devil. As
Hale explains, 'This is a strange time, Mister. No man may
longer doubt the powers of the dark are gathered in monstrous
attack upon this village. There is too much evidence now to
deny it' (Miller 1957, p. 272).

In the face of such beliefs, any suggestion that the actions of
the court were based on a 'fraud' would be construed as one
further element in the conspiracy, which Hale a little later
describes as a 'misty plot . . . so subtle we should be criminal to
cling to old respects and ancient friendships' (Miller 1957, p.
277). What is in fact emerging in Salem is a kind of state-
sanctioned paranoia which McCarthy tried to establish in the
United States, and which in recent times assumed its most
extreme form in National Socialist Germany.

It is of vital importance to an understanding of *The Crucible* to
see that Miller was concerned with the emergence of paranoia
as an officially held and promulgated belief capable of producing within society the new 'subjective reality' which he describes as having emerged in the early 1950s. Robert Welch, the
retired candy manufacturer, is a relatively harmless figure
within a society which has managed to retain intact its ability to
separate fantasy from fact. His visions of communists taking

over the Pentagon and the CIA can be relied upon, in such circumstances, to provide the liberal press with a degree of light relief. In the late 1940s and 1950s, however, the situation was closer to that presented in *The Crucible* than many contemporary observers were prepared to admit.

A single but pertinent indication of what was happening to concepts of 'reality' can be found in the testimony given by Bertolt Brecht before the House Un-American Activities Committee in 1947, when it was investigating 'The Communist Infiltration of The Motion Picture Industry' (see Firestone 1972, pp. 133–63). Robert Stripling, chief investigator for the Committee, led into a line of argument which seemed designed to permit Brecht's anti-Nazi works to be regarded as un-American: 'Mr Brecht, is it true that you have written a number of very revolutionary poems, plays, and other writings?' Brecht's reply was as follows: 'I have written a number of poems and songs and plays in the fight against Hitler and, of course, they can be considered, therefore, as revolutionary because I, of course, was for the overthrow of that government' (Firestone 1972, p. 143). In fairness, one must add that the Chairman of the Committee thereupon instructed Stripling that Brecht's anti-German activities were of no interest. Had he admitted such interest, he would no doubt have been forced to take into the record of the hearings a lengthy and eloquent statement which Brecht had prepared beforehand, and which analyses events in pre-war Germany, especially the suppression of free cultural expression and the widespread use of the term 'un-German'. The statement was excluded from the hearing on the grounds that 'it is a very interesting story of German life but it is not at all pertinent to this inquiry' (Firestone 1972, p. 139).

The principle according to which Brecht's experiences in Germany were declared irrelevant suggests why Miller was drawn to records of early American history in his attempts to illumine aspects of the present. The paranoia of other nations and societies, expressing itself as it must through an arbitrary and culturally distanced interpretive system, is more readily seen through by an outside observer than by an active participant in the communicative process. The various authority figures in government, or in institutions such as education and the Church, will tend to reinforce respect for certain beliefs only when we are willing to identify with the authority they represent or when that authority can be used directly within a behaviouristic system of reward and punishment in order to manipulate opinion.

The point need not be developed in detail here; one need think only of the emotive meaning of the word 'Hitler' for, on the one hand, those soldiers who swore an oath of allegiance to him, and on the other, the millions of British and American viewers whose imaginations had been shaped by Chaplin's film *The Great Dictator*. By selecting colonial Massachusetts, rather than, say, Germany in the 1930s, as the milieu for a dramatic presentation of deep moral and political issues, Miller certainly was able to avoid the kind of pragmatic-emotive interference which would have played a role in an American audience's reception of the image 'Germany' in the 1950s.

Early America, so often extolled by conservative spokesmen as an Arcadia of moral integrity and deeply held values, possessed its own emotive connotations which might, in fact, render the moral implications of the drama even more compelling. An 'inexplicable darkness' in the very heart of early New England, illuminated and analysed through the interplay of recognizable characters with familiar names, might well be the very stuff capable of 'unveiling a truth already known but unrecognized as such' (Miller 1957, p. 11). And characters like John Proctor and Giles Corey, hard-working and outspoken farmers carving out an existence for themselves and their descendants at the edge of the New World, would surely seem to represent in quintessential form the values upon which many Americans see their country as being founded. Their clash with established authority might appear capable of at least suggesting that their individualism be interpreted through the eyes of Thoreau, and not be seen merely as a residue of common sense in a society whose outdated and hence irrelevant superstitutions were beginning to run wild. That *The Crucible* did not by and large meet with such understanding is regrettable, but hardly surprising in view of the fact that what Miller perceived as being 'in the air' in the 1950s would inevitably influence the critical reception of his play.

In this regard it might be rewarding to compare the portrayal of authority in *The Crucible* with that to be found in the filmed version of James Jones's novel *From Here to Eternity*, which appeared in 1953, the year in which *The Crucible* was first performed. Individualism and the questioning of authority are presented in the film as being directed primarily against low and medium level figures in the army hierarchy. Injustices are perpetrated only because the upper elements, the benevolent Supreme Court of Hollywood mythology in the 1950s, are uninformed as to what is happening. The dissonances set in motion by the film are resolved by having the sadistic stockade sergeant stabbed to death by one of the individualists, while the 'bad' commanding officer is finally unmasked and disciplined by higher authorities. *From Here to Eternity*, one suspects, served to perpetuate and affirm precisely the attitudes towards authority which Arthur Miller set out to question and indeed to undermine in *The Crucible*. Central aspects of the critics' response to *The Crucible* certainly reveal an inability, if not a downright unwillingness, to discuss or apparently even to grasp the play's deep and immediate topical significance.

The Crucible was first performed at the Martin Beck theatre in New York, on 22 January 1953. The first-night audience received the play tumultuously and enthusiastically, according it nineteen curtain calls and insisting that the author appear on the stage to accept in person the shouts of 'Bravo' which echoed throughout the house. An auspicious beginning indeed, and one which seemed to guarantee a long run. The play closed in fact in July, after a total of 197 performances, compared to the 328 of *All My Sons* and the 742 performances of *Death of a Salesman*, which ran for almost two years at the Morosco Theatre.

The reviews which appeared shortly after the opening performance of *The Crucible* differed sharply in their assessment of the play, not merely in their evaluation of its artistic merits, but also in their elucidation of the meaning and significance of the drama. Against the political background of the early 1950s one would assume there could be little doubt that the critics would perceive the persecution of the Salem 'witches' depicted in the play as a 'message' which was both intended, by the outspoken liberal Arthur Miller, and received, by the applauding New York audience, as a commentary on the anti-communist witch-hunting activities of Joseph McCarthy and his followers. Yet many critics betrayed great reluctance to discuss this aspect of the drama, and some even attempted to deny that it existed.

Robert Coleman, for example, writing in the *Daily Mirror* (New York) of 23 January 1953, stresses the play's melodramatic appeal, advises 'tired businessmen' to 'try a revue' rather than *The Crucible*, and concludes with the following statement:

> Some may try to read into it more than we suspect is there. If there are deep implications in the script for modern playgoers we failed to find them. Just take it as a stirring melodrama acted to the hilt. (Coleman 1953)

John Chapman, writing for the *Daily News* (23 January 1953), came to similar conclusions. A summary of the plot and some comments on individual actors are accompanied by the following words concerning the play's 'implications':

> However, those who may have expected Miller, an admitted liberal, to make a political parable of this play – as he did with (his adaptation of) Ibsen's *An Enemy of the People* – will have to read into *The Crucible* their own implications, for the piece is just what it sets out to be: a tragic drama about the historic Puritan purge of witchcraft. (Chapman 1953)

Some critics at the time almost give the impression that they are using their columns as a means of protecting themselves from accusations that they might indeed have experienced the kind of reception which Coleman and Chapman declare to be inappropriate yet decline to explain. John McClain, for example, writing in *Journal American* (23 January 1953), claimed that the actions performed by the characters in *The Crucible* were so incredible that he found it impossible to relate them to anything in his realm of personal experience: 'Okay, it happened. But it is so far beyond our present concepts of justice and plausible behavior that I never felt myself part of the proceedings. . . . I only wish he'd written it around people more presently understandable.' When he left the theatre, McClain 'was not greatly moved by anything that had happened'. Eleven years later, however, when the play was revived on Broadway, McClain reviewed it once more for *Journal American* and found it to provide 'a most moving evening in the theater' (7 April 1964). One is forced to wonder what the demise of McCarthyism had contributed to McClain's new judgement, especially in view of the fact that in 1964, far from denying that Miller's characters *can* be related to contemporary persons, he suggests that this is precisely what he had been doing in 1953 when he denied that it was possible: 'I always thought Mr. Arthur Miller, the author, made a ridiculously patent case against the judiciary, and I wasn't prepared to go along with the insinuation that the situation hadn't been much improved in the intervening centuries' (*Journal American*, 7 April 1964).

Not all reviewers were prepared to deny that *The Crucible* possessed 'implications' or contemporary relevance. Brooks Atkinson, writing in the *New York Times*, stated flatly, 'Neither Mr. Miller nor his audiences are unaware of certain similarities between the perversions of justice then and today' (23 January 1953). A review in the *New Yorker* of 31 January 1953, regarded *The Crucible* as being 'on its primary level, a play about the Salem witch trials in 1692', whereas, 'on its secondary and contemporary level, of course, Mr. Miller's piece says that witch-hunting is still among the most popular of American pastimes'. John Mason Brown, in his piece entitled 'Witch-hunting' written for *Saturday Review* (14 February 1953), admits the validity of such interpretation in his remark, 'the likenesses between the past and present are disquietingly clear', but he severely restricts the significance of his observation by claiming that Miller's attempted allegory rested on a metaphysical flaw:

> Witches never existed except in the imagination, but today there are traitors who have wormed their way into positions where they can do great harm. No one can dispute the need for spotting and removing them. The question is one of method. (Brown 1953)

In this battle among the critics for the meaning of *The Crucible* one of the most remarkable assaults on Miller was delivered by Robert Warshow in his article, 'The Liberal Conscience in *The Crucible*: Arthur Miller and his Audience' (*Commentary*, March 1953). Warshow, unlike such critics as Coleman and Chapman, makes no attempt to deny *The Crucible* its implications or its timeliness; on the contrary he addresses himself to just this aspect of the drama so as to comment unfavourably on the political motivations and beliefs of those who shouted 'Bravo' at the New York performances.

Warshow's basic argument was familiar enough at the time and could be summarized thus: allegorical implications inhere in the play, but they are misplaced because there are no real similarities between the so-called witch-hunting of the early 1950s and that which led to the Salem trial; the witches of Salem were innocent while communists are not. The trials depicted in *The Crucible*, Warshow suggests further,

> were much more like the trial that just ended in Prague than like any trial that has lately taken place in the United States. . . . And yet I cannot believe that it was for this particular implication that anyone shouted 'Bravo!' (Warshow 1953, p. 268)

Miller's main characteristic as a writer is his 'refusal of complexity, the assured simplicity of his view of human behavior'. *Death of a Salesman* was 'impressively confusing', and indeed the universality of Arthur Miller 'belongs neither to literature nor to history, but to that journalism of limp erudition which assumes that events are to be understood by referring them to categories'. One of the most interesting aspects of *The Crucible*, for Warshow, was that it 'offers us a revealing glimpse of the way the Communists and their fellow-travelers have come to regard themselves' (Warshow 1953, p. 270).

These commentaries by Warshow and others are fascinating and significant for several reasons. First of all, the contemporary reception of *The Crucible*, producing as it did essential interpretative disagreements only a few hours after the first performance, could be seen as a concentrated microcosm of some of the more leisurely disagreements which have spanned decades and centuries of, say, construing the meaning of *Hamlet*. The very nature of the disagreements, moreover, throws into question the narrowness of a historicism which would assume and attempt to reconstruct the unified understanding of a work's postulated 'immediate audience'. Above all, however, the reviews force our attention to the network of ideology and persuasion which accompanies a literary work's reception, and which can influence and modify in a number of important ways the manner in which the work is to be related to the personal experiences of the recipient.

Academic criticism in the United States, it must be remembered, was in the early 1950s dominated by the doctrines of New Criticism; the contemporary relevance of *The Crucible*, in so far as it might be admitted at all to such discussion, would have been swiftly impoverished by being assimilated into a cosmic scheme of 'universal significance' and hence universal persecution. New York audiences, on the other hand, were clearly in no mood to permit their immediate response to the play to be limited according to the types of evidence which the New Critics might have declared appropriate. The spontaneous applause which greeted John Proctor's question – 'Is the accuser always holy now' (Miller 1957, p. 281) – was obviously prompted by the belief that the word 'now' referred to 1953 at least as much as to 1692. Coleman, Chapman and McClain, by denying that such an understanding was 'in the text', were not merely urging upon their readers a New Critical or strictly historical approach; they were also dissociating themselves from any suspicion or indeed accusation that they themselves might even fleetingly have engaged in such thoughts.

But the audiences continued to shout 'Bravo!' in spite of their admonitions. Robert Warshow thereupon took it upon himself to demonstrate that the shouts signified at best a simple-minded liberalism, and at worst an unpatriotic and sinister belief in the innocence of such people as Alger Hiss. Popular criticism thus reveals itself as a kind of secondary censorship attempting to suppress not the publication of the text so much as meanings which 'naive' audiences or readers might be inclined to attach to the text. Warshow seems to possess some awareness of this process of thought control, for in commenting on the deliberate vagueness of Miller's allegorizing, he asks: 'How can he be held responsible for what comes into my head while I watch his play?' (Warshow 1953, p. 269). In other words, a spectator who finds himself indulging in meanings proscribed by Warshow will not be permitted to excuse himself by pointing to authorial intention *or* textual structure; the meanings will be his, the recipient's, and his will be the duty of defending them. Two letters expressing disagreement with Warshow's analysis were published in a later issue of *Commentary* (July 1953, p. 83), and it is somewhat troubling to note that both correspondents found it necessary to qualify their disagreement by stating that they certainly did not doubt the guilt of Alger Hiss.

Both in substance and rhetoric, these contemporary arguments about the meaning of *The Crucible* reflect in an almost uncanny way the events and realities represented in the play itself. We find ourselves in both cases dealing with matters of perception, interpretation, authority, intimidation and speculation concerning honesty of motive. The question of authority and the individual's relation to it is particularly important, for it is clear that both Warshow and Miller are concerned with the kind of authority which cannot merely make people act in a certain way, but which can also force them to perceive and interpret in a certain way. An examination of concepts of authority in *The Crucible*, moreover, is likely to shed light on the allegations that the play is fundamentally propaganda in a superficial and dishonest sense, as suggested by Warshow. What many contemporary critics found disconcerting and 'propagandistic', I suspect, was not so much any openly political message which they accused others of reading into the drama, but rather the innate capacity of art to subvert, sometimes by questioning directly the wisdom and the source of authority of those forces which shape our concept and experience of 'reality'.

The Crucible, as Miller indicates at the very beginning of the play, depicts a society which possessed a tenuous and uneasy relationship to realities of various kinds. For purposes of social and political order, a theocracy had established itself in Salem, 'to keep the community together, and to prevent any kind of disunity that might open it to destruction by material or ideological enemies' (Miller 1957, p. 228). The stability of such a system, founded upon repression and autocracy, was threatened not only by individual outbreaks of political or religious heresy; it also had to reckon with the psychological frailty of a community which inhabited 'the edge of the wilderness'. The American continent was 'full of mystery' for the early settlers of Massachusetts: 'It stood, dark and threatening over their shoulders night and day, for out of it Indian tribes marauded from time to time' (Miller 1957, p. 227). To the best of their knowledge, Miller continues, 'the American forest was the last place on earth that was not paying homage to God' (Miller 1957, p. 227).

The authorities of Salem, thus armed with exact knowledge

concerning the geographical boundary at which Christian good gave way to impenetrable darkness, were perhaps understandably deluded into believing that they could chart the topography of the soul with a similar precision. 'The Devil', Hale assures those who would trespass on his expert knowledge, 'is precise; the marks of his presence are definite as stone' (Miller 1957, p. 252). It is no coincidence that the episode which set in motion the trials and persecution – Parris's discovery of his daughter and niece 'dancing like heathen in the forest' (Miller 1957, p. 231) – draws together the manifold strands of repressed sexuality, rebelliousness and the half-conscious notion that the enemy within was somehow to be identified with the unexplored terrain which began in the forest.

More exactly it is the interpretation of this episode rather than the act itself which initiates the troubles, for a dispute as to its meaning quickly separates Rebecca Nurse, John Proctor and others who regard the incident as an excess of childish mischief, from those such as Parris who wish to view it as evidence that the Devil is loose in Salem. The supporters of Parris, for reasons ranging from personal profit, to malice, to a genuine dread of blasphemous practices, insist on having the whole matter explained and dealt with authoritatively. The depiction of this authority – its nature and workings, the logic upon which it rests, its savage intrusion into the life of John Proctor – forms one of the central features of *The Crucible*. I shall conclude the present discussion by investigating certain facets of the relationship between Proctor and authority, in particular the series of events which culminates in his being able to triumph morally over the court even while it crushes him physically.

In the first act of the play John Proctor reveals himself as an empiricist; his trust in his own experiences, observations and feelings is matched by a deep suspicion of abstractions and hierarchies of authority which seem to contradict individual common sense. His democratic leanings – 'We vote by name in this society, not by acreage' (Miller 1957, p. 245) – signify a willingness to believe that others will make correct moral choices provided their judgement is not obscured by matters of self-interest. What Proctor does find difficult to comprehend is that others will do wrong not merely when prompted by recognizable motives such as greed or desire to escape punishment, but because they have chosen to suppress or distort the reality of personal feeling by appealing to external systems of authority. The potential heresy of such thought within a theocracy is brought out clearly in the following exchange:

> PARRIS: There is either obedience or the church will burn like Hell is burning!
> PROCTOR: Can you speak one minute without we land in Hell again? I am sick of Hell!
> PARRIS: It is not for you to say what is good for you to hear!
> PROCTOR: I may speak my heart, I think!
> PARRIS, *in a fury*: What, are we Quakers? We are not Quakers here yet, Mr. Proctor. And you may tell that to your followers!
> PROCTOR: My followers!
> PARRIS – *now he's out with it*: There is a party in this church. I am not blind; there is a faction and a party.
> PROCTOR: Against you?
> PUTNAM: Against him and all authority!
> PROCTOR: Why, then I must find it and join it.
> > *There is shock among the others.*
> REBECCA: He does not mean that.
> PUTNAM: He confessed it now!
> PROCTOR: I mean it solemnly, Rebecca; I like not the smell of this 'authority'. (Miller 1957, p. 246)

Against the background of these words there is a certain ominous symbolism in the arrival a little later of Reverend Hale, the expert on witchcraft. He is carrying six heavy books which, he explains in words which excite a sense of fear in Parris, are 'weighted with authority' (Miller 1957, p. 251). Yet Parris's anxiety soon subsides once he realizes that the presence of Hale together with the tangible authority of his knowledge can be made to sanction his own interpretations of events. The confession is now no longer an inadvertent sign of unorthodox thought, to be seized upon in conversation as in the passage cited above; it becomes the last formal element of a process designed to force the confessing person to legitimize the already authoritatively established explanation of his actions and mental states. 'You will confess yourself', Parris informs Tituba, 'or

I will take you out and whip you to your death' (Miller 1957, p. 257).

The logic of paranoia is beginning to take over. When Mary Warren returns home after a day in court, she demands civil treatment not because she has any real claim to it, but because she sat to dinner with four judges and the King's deputy. Parris's actions are to be judged authoritatively and not according to observation: 'The man's ordained, therefore the light of God is in him' (Miller 1957, p. 273). The fact that the gaols are crowded is seen not as a *result* of persecution but as a natural *reason* for continuing with it: 'The jails are packed – our greatest judges sit in Salem now – and hangin's promised. Man, we must look to cause proportionate' (Miller 1957, p. 282). Danforth, the judge who would 'hang ten thousand that dared to rise against the law' (Miller 1957, p. 318), cannot be fallible for 'near to four hundred are in the jails from Marblehead to Lynn' upon his signature, and 'seventy-two condemned to hang by that signature' (Miller 1957, p. 188).

The madness of forcing the event to fit the explanation, rather than vice-versa, is brought out vividly in the scene where Elizabeth Proctor shocks Hale and confuses her husband by stating that she cannot believe in witches: 'If you think that I am one, then I say there are none' (Miller 1957, p. 276). In a piece of dramatic irony which foreshadows Hale's later insight into the truth, Miller permits the interrogator to take over the same proposition a few moments later: 'Believe me, Mr. Nurse, if Rebecca Nurse be tainted, then nothing's left to stop the whole green world from burning' (Miller 1957, p. 277). In the final act, when Hale is desperately urging Elizabeth to prevail upon her husband to save his life by confessing to a lie, there is no longer any doubt in Elizabeth's mind concerning the true nature of the court and its henchmen: 'I think that be the Devil's argument' (Miller 1957, p. 320).

The supreme moral triumph is reserved for John Proctor in his final confrontation with Danforth. Proctor's ultimate vision of clarity and truth was not lightly attained, and would surely be cheapened if it were regarded as a straightforward and predictable outcome of his contempt for sham authority. While it is true that he derives his moral sense from his own very direct and basic experience of reality and from his insistence on 'proof', we are still presented with glimpses of a man who finds it difficult to reconcile the authenticity of his feelings with his knowledge of how others think.

The affair with Abigail, for example, troubles him not because he himself attaches much significance to it, but because he is conscious of having committed what others, in particular his wife, regard as a sin. His moral perplexity is most evident in the first part of Act Two, where we witness the inner struggle of a person seeking to comprehend the reality of a judgement which finds little echo in his own feelings. On this level of meaning, his references to nature – 'I think we'll see green fields soon. It's warm as blood beneath the clods. . . Lilacs have a purple smell. Lilac is the smell of nightfall I think. Massachusetts is a beauty in the spring' (Miller 1957, p. 262) – seem to represent an attempt to establish an external basis in reality which would confirm and somehow authenticate his feelings. It is certainly revealing to compare such imagery, based on personal experience, with the language of Danforth, for whom nature is simply a metaphorical stage-setting for an *a priori* view of reality: 'We live no longer in the dusky afternoon when evil mixed with good and befuddled the world. Now, by God's grace, the shining sun is up, and them that fear not light will surely praise it' (Miller 1957, p. 293).

The pathos of Act Three, where a muted and anxious Proctor pleads with Danforth for his wife's life, is certainly deepened by our consciousness of this contrast between the very core of the two men, and by our knowledge that the position of authority held by one is forcing the other to betray his own self. In the final clash between the two, however, the victory belongs to Proctor, for when he refuses to sign a confession, saying to Danforth, 'You are the high court, your word is good enough' (Miller 1957, p. 327), he has at last achieved a clearsighted awareness of the worth of his own moral being. The word of the high court, as both he and Danforth now know, is not good enough, despite all the extraneous authority with which it might be endowed.

Twenty years later, as Arthur Miller added in his postscript to the play, 'the power of theocracy in Massachusetts was broken' (Miller 1957, p. 330). It is well worth asking, as Miller did in *The Crucible*, what role was played by people such as John Proctor in bringing the madness to an end, and what relevance the events and Miller's interpretation of them might hold for a particular audience. The readers or spectators of today, as opposed to those of 1953, have an additional dimension of significance to consider, for they are in a position to assess the applicability of Miller's vision to a further thirty years of American history. Some events in this period suggest that while Miller's unmasking of authority and awed co-operation with it reflected accurately certain underlying social truths, the major-ity of Americans preferred to believe in the myth of supreme benevolence fabricated for mass consumption in such films as *From Here to Eternity*.

The dramatic and moral power of *The Crucible* is undeniable, but its demystifying effectiveness within a given historical situation remains ultimately difficult to assess. Twenty-one years after its first performance an American president appeared on television to proclaim to the world that he was not 'a crook'. The events which led to this crisis suggest that an adversary rhetoric, even in its non-literary manifestations, is no longer capable of influencing political events more than margin-ally. Paul Corcoran, in his recent study of the political implica-tions of post-literate societies, has reminded us that rhetorical protests against the Vietnam war in America, even when they became vociferous mass demonstrations, 'were clearly unper-suasive to the public at large, who broadly accepted, not the government's own rhetoric (which was blithely assumed to be riddled with "credibility gaps"), but the offices and identities of those in power' (Corcoran 1979, p. 174).

The recognition of this truth need not lead to pessimism, for in the act of recognizing it we have prepared the basis of resistance against Ellul's fear that we will be destroyed by propaganda. In this sense *The Crucible* becomes important not simply in terms of its effectiveness as specific historical demys-tification, but as an example of what Noam Chomsky once described with refreshing simplicity as the responsibility of intellectuals: 'To speak the truth and to expose lies' (Chomsky 1968, p. 269).

Many reviewers of *The Crucible* in 1953, as we have seen, were not prepared to admit that Miller was speaking the truth and exposing lies. They questioned the truthfulness of his vision of early New England, and denied that this vision – even if it were accepted as reflecting historical truth – should be permitted to function as an interpretant capable of producing a new understanding of the present. The chorus of disapproval has of course been subdued by the fact that *The Crucible* is now widely regarded as one of the most compelling plays of the twentieth century. This does not mean that Arthur Miller won the propaganda battle, for the readiness of present-day critics to see the play as a courageous stand against McCarthyism introduces a fresh propagandist dimension; the play proves that defiance and free speech were possible, it serves as an alibi for those who refused to speak out. An attack on the system thus becomes a vindication of it, and John Proctor's martyrdom is transformed into the guarantor of Miller's (and our) democratic rights. To the extent that *The Crucible* is received as a national myth it will lose its demystifying power. 'Democracy', in the words of Jacques Ellul, 'cannot be an object of faith, of belief: it is an expression of opinions. . . . To make a myth of democracy is to present the opposite of democracy' (Ellul 1973, p. 244).

10

Conclusion

In order to confront literature with propaganda, and to describe the points at which the one process may be seen to be reinforcing or questioning the other, we need to challenge a number of partial but widespread definitions of both concepts. First of all, it must be recognized that neither literature nor propaganda can be defined adequately in the terms of any one of the many communicative aspects involved, including authorial intention, message form, textual designata, actual reception and hypothetical reception. In addition, the point at which literature becomes propaganda or demystification can be described only when we accept that literature functions communicatively within specific historical and cultural systems of discourse.

While this clearly does not mean that literature can be explicated only by investigating the discourses within which a particular text was historically produced and received, it does imply a rejection of the notion that the essence of literature should be seen as a sort of aesthetic timelessness which has the power to speak to us across the ages. The very concept of timelessness, if it is to represent more than a personal and unprovable value judgement, can derive only from a succession of accumulating acts of reception, each one of which is subject to its own historicity. In recognizing this historicity, and in accepting that our own consciousness as readers is likewise determined by a variety of historical factors, we have the beginnings of a dialectical perspective from which literature, and indeed all sign processes, can be observed when they operate in a propagandistic or demystifying way. The modes of perception which texts may produce, affirm or subvert must be understood as specific interpretative systems for dealing with reality, economic relationships, social formations, human behaviour, political institutions and so on. State controllers of literature, whether they act to censor texts or to promote certain types of text, have always assumed this relationship between literature and life. Methods of mediating literature which deny it do not thereby protect literature from the censors, and can in fact themselves become accomplices to the processes of propaganda. It is significant that some recent examples of a demystifying literature have attempted to devise strategies for anticipating and resisting the capacity of aestheticism to absorb and neutralize messages.

Although there is no ready-made method for detecting propaganda, we can become aware of the general categories in which it manifests itself and we can attempt to classify its techniques and forms. Literature can assist us in this, not merely because it is able to function both as propaganda and anti-propaganda, but also because its existence as preserved discourse permits us to investigate the historicity of one form of human communication. This approach does not mean that we must study literature as a set of documents rather than as a set of aesthetic objects. For in effect it denies the validity of such a distinction by assuming that the propagandistic or demystifying moment of literary communication may be inseparable from its aesthetic function. This point of intersection will be historically determined but it should not be regarded as a frozen act of past communication which only philological and historical reconstruction can set free. Earlier literary texts, with and without 'semiotic guerilla warfare', constantly reveal their capacity to enter into new systems of signifying. The custodians of literature who insist on consigning their texts to a room marked 'Middle Ages' or 'seventeenth century' distort this dimension of meaning just as surely as do those who attempt to detach the texts from history altogether.

From the point of view of propaganda analysis, historical methods are undeniably valuable when they successfully reconstruct the modes of perception which a given text can be observed to have affirmed or challenged. But they become misleading when they insist that these modes of perception must be identified for all time with the reconstructed interpretants of the author's immediate contemporary readership. If we adapt the historical method, and see it as a means of reconstructing the relationship between textual structure and reception wherever and whenever it may occur, we might provide the base for a critical method which will treat literature as preserved discourse and not as mummified discourse. To the extent that such a method will transform the critic into the observer of an actual sign process, it may also lead to a clearer understanding of the ways in which literature functions as propaganda.

This approach will not unmask propaganda universally, however. It is all too easy to 'detect' propaganda when we are distanced, not historically but politically, from acts of communication, and from modes of perception which we attribute to speakers and hearers. Western readers tend to 'see through' *Pravda*. If they subscribe to the *Guardian* they probably regard *The Sun* as propaganda for the masses. Few people today would be likely to succumb to the spell of such Nazi poets as Baldur von Schirach and Heinrich Anacker, and even Goody Two-shoes has been demystified by popular semantic acclamation. The propaganda which is most elusive, and which for that reason is most in need of detection, is not the one we observe but the one which succeeds in engaging us directly as participants in its communicative systems. The study of literary texts, which through the centuries have served the purposes of both propaganda and demystification, provide us with the possibility of investigating various aspects of this process. I shall conclude by expressing the hope that a reformed system of literary education will acknowledge this possibility, both as a fact and a challenge.

Notes on
further reading

The following notes contain suggestions for those readers wishing to pursue further some of the main concepts and topics treated in the earlier sections. Titles discussed below in abbreviated form have been referred to in the preceding text, and are listed in full in the *Bibliography*.

Propaganda

The literature on propaganda, which ranges from the highly conjectural to the precisely empirical, is already vast and continues to accumulate rapidly. Walter Dieckmann (1975) *Sprache in der Politik. Einführung in die Pragmatik und Semantik der politischen Sprache* (Heidelberg) lists in his bibliography hundreds of titles, mainly German, which appeared between 1969 and 1975. A readily accessible but very broad introduction is J. A. C. Brown (1963) *Techniques of Persuasion. From Propaganda to Brainwashing* (Harmondsworth, Middx: Penguin Books). The titles below represent 'standard' accounts (Doob), popular approaches (Packard, Whyte) and scientific/empirical studies (Rosnow/Robinson):

Doob, Leonard W. (1948) *Public Opinion and Propaganda* (New York).
Ellul, Jacques (1964) *The Technological Society*, trans. by John Wilkinson (New York).
Katz, Daniel, Cartwright, Dorwin, Eldersveld, Samuel J. and Lee, Alfred McClung (eds) (1954) *Public Opinion and Propaganda* (New York).
Lazarsfeld, Paul F., Berelson, Bernard and Gaudet, Hazel (1960) *The People's Choice* (New York).

Lerner, Daniel (ed.) (1961) *Propaganda in War and Crisis* (New York).

Packard, Vance O. (1957) *The Hidden Persuaders* (New York).

Rosnow, Ralph L., and Robinson, Edward J. (eds) (1967) *Experiments in Persuasion* (New York).

Schramm, Wilbur L. (1948) *Communication in Modern Society* (Urbana, Ill.).

Whyte, William H. (1956) *The Organization Man* (New York).

An account of the research commissioned by the US Army's Information and Educational Division in the last war can be found in Carl I. Hovland, Arthur A. Lumsdaine and Fred D. Sheffield (1949) *Experiments on Mass Communication* (Princeton, NJ). The authors were interested in such questions as how 'better educated men' might be induced to accept certain beliefs (pp. 224–5). Some of the peace-time follow-up applications of such research are suggested in Carl I. Hovland, Irving L. Janis and Harold H. Kelley (1953) *Communication and Persuasion – Psychological Studies of Opinion Change* (New Haven, Conn.). The study is introduced with the note that 'Executives in many organizations feel the need to improve their communication systems in order to achieve widespread acceptance of the standards and values necessary to the success of their enterprises' (Hovland, Janis and Kelley 1953, p. 1).

Ellul (1973) was used extensively by me for two reasons: his categories can be applied readily to literary communication; his treatment is broadly inclusive, touching upon politics, advertising, revolutionary situations, social institutions, etc.

Literature

Modern critical traditions and approaches have been discussed with authority and erudition by René Wellek (1955 onwards) *A History of Modern Criticism* (New Haven, Conn.); four of the projected five volumes have appeared. David Lodge (ed.) (1972) *20th Century Literary Criticism* (London) has brought together a wide-ranging representative collection of critical modes and theories. The section on Marxist criticism is thin, and should be augmented by Solomon (1979) and Berel Lang and Forrest Williams (eds) (1972) *Marxism and Art: Writings in Aesthetics and Criticism* (New York). Before embarking on a detailed study of the extremely divergent forms of contemporary Marxist aesthetics, the reader might want to look first at Karl Marx and Friedrich Engels (1947) *Literature and Art* (New York); it should be noted that the German edition, Manfred Kliem (ed.) (1967) *Über Kunst und Literatur*, 2 vols (Berlin), is more comprehensive than the English translation. Important political interpretations of these sources can be studied in:

V. I. Lenin (1967) *On Literature and Art* (Moscow);
L. Trotsky (1971) *Literature and Revolution* (Ann Arbor, Mich.);
Mao Tse-Tung (1967) *On Literature and Art* (Peking).

Apart from Szanto (1978) very little has been written specifically on literature and propaganda. However, many useful insights can be gained from the numerous studies on literature and politics, ideology, society, etc. Charles I. Glicksberg (1976) *The Literature of Commitment* (London), is sweeping and impressively detailed, but like Rühle (1969) it bristles with liberal indignation and must be approached with caution. Other works of interest include:

Brown, Malcolm (1972) *The Politics of Irish Literature: From Thomas Davis to W. B. Yeats* (London).
Dickinson, H. T. (ed.) (1974) *Politics and Literature in the Eighteenth Century* (London).
Ingle, Stephen (1979) *Socialist Thought in Imaginative Literature* (London).
Knights, Lionel C. (1954) *Poetry, Politics and the English Tradition* (London).
Lucas, John (ed.) (1971) *Literature and Politics in the Nineteenth Century* (London).
Morris, John A. (1977) *Writers and Politics in Modern Britain 1880–1950* (London).
Watson, George (1977) *Politics and Literature in Modern Britain* (London).

Studies with a greater emphasis on political and social theory, ideology, etc., are:

Adorno, Theodor W. (1974) *Noten zur Literatur* (Frankfurt).
Benjamin, Walter (1969) in Hannah Arendt (ed.), *Illuminations* (New York).
Eagleton, Terry (1976) *Marxism and Literary Criticism* (London).
Enzensberger, Hans Magnus, 'The consciousness industry', in *New Left Review*, 64, (November–December 1970), 13–39.
Fischer, Ernest (1969) *Art Against Ideology*, trans. by Anna Bostock (Harmondsworth, Middx: Penguin Books).
Hauser, Arnold (1951) *The Social History of Art* (New York).
Jameson, Fredric (1971) *Marxism and Form* (Princeton, NJ).
Lifschitz, Mikhail (1938) *The Philosophy of Art of Karl Marx* (New York).
Macherey, Pierre (1978) *A Theory of Literary Production*, trans. by Geoffrey Wall (London).

Sartre, Jean-Paul (1967) *What is Literature?* (London).
Stein, Peter (ed.) (1973) *Theorie der politischen Dichtung* (Munich).

Many of the historical and specific literary/political issues mentioned in various sections have attracted a vast secondary literature of their own. The cultural and publishing policies of National Socialism are well documented by Strothmann (1963) and discussed by Taylor (1980) and Brenner (1963). Sander L. Gilman (ed.) (1971) *NS-Literaturtheorie: eine Dokumentation* (Frankfurt) is a useful anthology of the theoretical statements of National Socialism. In addition to Balfour (1979) an account of Nazi propaganda can be found in Z. A. B. Zeman (1964) *Nazi Propaganda* (Oxford). Hans Wagener (ed.) (1977) *Gegenwartsliteratur und Drittes Reich* (Stuttgart) is a useful collection of essays discussing the relationship of post-war literature to National Socialism, while Horst Denkler and Karl Prümm (eds) (1976) *Die Deutsche Literatur im Dritten Reich* (Stuttgart) contains a number of excellent critical investigations into Nazi literature itself.

Emmerich (1981) is the best and most up-to-date exposition of the cultural politics of the GDR. An interesting East German account of western criticism as anti-communist propaganda can be found in Hermann Kähler (1974) *Der kalte Krieg der Kritiker, Zur antikommunistischen Kritik an der DDR-Literatur* (Berlin). Peter Hutchinson (1977) *Literary Presentations of Divided Germany* (Cambridge, England) has investigated the East German fictional treatment up to 1970 of an important political issue. John Flores (1971) *Poetry in East Germany* (New Haven, Conn.) has written a sensitive account of the lyric in the same period. The drama has been discussed from an interesting perspective by Katherine Vanovitch (1981) 'Female roles in East German drama 1949–1977' (unpubl. PhD diss. Cambridge, England). There is little of a general nature in English, but the journals *GDR Monitor* (Dundee) and *New German Critique* (Milwaukee) contain much relevant and valuable material. For those who read German, Hans Koch *et al.* (eds) (1974) *Zur Theorie des sozialistischen Realismus* (Berlin) provides fascinating insights into post-revolutionary and post-Stalinist aesthetics. In its 914 pages the book is not surprisingly somewhat uneven, and the rapidity with which it reinstates Kafka twice and banishes him three times is downright confusing. More sophisticated is Manfred Naumann *et al.* (1975) *Gesellschaft, Literatur, Lesen: Literaturrezeption in theoretischer Sicht* (Berlin and Weimar), which takes a critical and probing look at reception theory.

A good introduction to reception theory and reader-response criticism is Jane P. Tompkins (ed.) (1980) *Reader-Response Criticism: From Formalism to Post-Structuralism* (Baltimore). The essays are representative and the book has an excellent annotated bibliography.

Children's fiction has attracted considerable attention in recent years. A good general history of the subject is Frederick J. Darton (1960) *Children's Books in England: Five Centuries of Social Life* (Cambridge, England). See also: Nicholas Tucker (ed.) (1976) *Suitable for Children? Controversies in Children's Literature* (London); A. Dorfmann and A. Mattelart (1975) *How to Read Donald Duck: Imperialist Ideology in the Disney Comic* (IG Editions); Mary Cadogan and Patricia Craig (1976) *You're a Brick Angela! A New Look at Girl's Fiction from 1839 to 1975* (London); Marcia R. Lieberman (1972) ' "Some day my prince will come": female acculturation through the fairy tale', *College English*, 34, 383–95. The last two titles are concerned additionally with sexist aspects of literature, further discussions of which can be found in: Elaine Showalter (ed.) (1971) *Women's Liberation and Literature* (New York); Barbara H. Rigney (1978) *Madness and Sexual Politics in the Feminist Novel: Studies in Bronte, Woolf, Lessing and Atwood* (Madison, Wis.); Patricia Stubbs (1979) *Women and Fiction: Feminism and the Novel 1880–1920* (Brighton, Sussex); Susan K. Cornillon (ed.) (1973) *Images of Women in Fiction: Feminist Perspectives* (Bowling Green, Ohio); Sidney J. Kaplan (1975) *Feminine Consciousness in the Modern British Novel* (Urbana, Ill.). An excellent and broad-ranging treatment of the subject is Lillian S. Robinson (1978) *Sex, Class and Culture* (Bloomington, Ind.).

Semiotics

The sign theories of Charles Morris, which have been freely adapted in the foregoing discussion, represent only one of the many semiotic ways of modelling propaganda as a process. I chose Morris because first of all he discusses literature and propaganda within the terms of his sign theories, and second because his concept of the interpretant provides the possibility of dealing with ideology without being inundated by the metaphysical abstractions characteristic of much contemporary discussion. Eco (1977) has a comprehensive bibliography of semiotics and communication theory. See also:

Elam, Keir (1980) *The Semiotics of Theatre and Drama* (London).
Greimas, A. J. *et al.* (eds) (1970) *Sign, Language, Culture* (The Hague).
Kristeva, Julia, Rey-Debove, Josette and Umiker, Donna Jean (eds) (1971) *Essays in Semiotics* (The Hague).
Matejka, Ladislav and Titunik, Irwin R. (eds) (1976) *Semiotics of Art: Prague School Contributions* (Cambridge, Mass.: MIT Press).
Peirce, Charles Sanders (1931–5, 1958, 1960) *Collected Papers*. 8 vols (Cambridge, Mass.).
Wienold, Götz (1972) *Semiotik der Literatur* (Frankfurt). Unfortunately

not available in English. See my review in *Comparative Literature* (1974), 2, 177–80.

Zima, Peter V. (ed.) (1977) *Textsemiotik als Ideologiekritik* (Frankfurt).

The Crucible

Weales (1977) has anthologized a useful cross-section of criticism on the play and its relation to history, though he does not include the immediate press reviews, which will have to be consulted directly. Other important background materials can be found in the following:

Frazier, Thomas R. (ed.) (1971) *The Underside of American History* (New York).

Matusow, Allen J. (ed.) (1970) *Joseph R. McCarthy* (Englewood Cliffs, NJ).

Moss, Leonard (1967) *Arthur Miller* (New York).

Murray, Robert K. (1955) *Red Scare: A Study of National Hysteria* (Minneapolis).

Preston, William (1966) *Aliens and Dissenters: Frederal Suppression of Radicals, 1903–1933* (New York).

Rogin, Michael Paul (1967) *The Intellectuals and McCarthy: The Radical Specter* (Cambridge, Mass.: MIT Press).

Strakey, Marion L. (1949) *The Devil in Massachusetts* (New York).

Welland, Dennis (1961) *Arthur Miller* (Edinburgh).

Bibliography

The following list contains only those titles referred to in the preceding discussion. Well-known literary works have not been included unless they were cited in a particular edition.

Bakhtin, Mikhail (1979) 'Laughter and freedom', in Maynard Solomon (ed.), *Marxism and Art* (Brighton, Sussex), 292–300.

Balfour, Michael (1979) *Propaganda in War 1939–1945* (London).

Barbusse, Henri (1917) *Under Fire* (New York).

Barthes, Roland (1972) *Mythologies*, trans. by Annette Lavers (New York).

Bateson, F. W. (1968) 'Linguistics and literary criticism', in Peter Demetz *et al.* (eds), *The Disciplines of Criticism* (New Haven, Conn.), 3–16.

Bell, Daniel (1976) *The Cultural Contradictions of Capitalism* (London).

Bellos, David (1980) review of Tony Bennett, *Formalism and Marxism*, *Journal of Literary Semantics*, IX/2, 121–2.

Belsey, Catherine (1980) *Critical Practice* (London).

Bennett, Tony (1979) *Formalism and Marxism* (London).

Booth, James (1981) *Writers and Politics in Nigeria* (London).

Booth, Wayne C. (1974) *Modern Dogma and the Rhetoric of Assent* (Notre Dame, Ind. and London).

Bowra, C. M. (1966) *Poetry and Politics 1900–1960* (Cambridge, England).

Brenner, Hildegard (1963) *Die Kunstpolitik des Nationalsozialismus* (Reinbek, W. Germany).

Brown, Edward J. (1969) *Russian Literature since the Revolution* (London).

Cherry, Colin (1978) *On Human Communication* (Cambridge, Mass.: MIT Press).

Chomsky, Noam (1968) 'The responsibility of intellectuals', in Theodore Roszak (ed.), *The Dissenting Academy* (New York), 254–98.

Corcoran, Paul E. (1979) *Political Language and Rhetoric* (Austin, Tex.).

Craig, David and Egan, Michael (1979) *Extreme Situations – Literature and Crisis From the Great War to the Atom Bomb* (London).

Craig, Gordon A. (1978) *Germany 1866–1945* (Oxford).

Dolan, Paul J. (1976) *Of War and War's Alarms: Fiction and Politics in the Modern World* (New York).

Eagleton, Terry (1976) *Criticism and Ideology* (London).

Eco, Umberto (1977) *A Theory of Semiotics* (London).

Ellmann, Mary (1979) *Thinking About Women* (London).

Ellul, Jacques (1973) *Propaganda: The Formation of Men's Attitudes*, trans. by Konrad Kellen and Jean Lerner (New York: Vintage Books).

Emmerich, Wolfgang (1981) *Kleine Literaturgeschichte der DDR* (Darmstadt, W. Germany).

Ermolaev, Herman (1963) *Soviet Literary Theories (1917–1934). The Genesis of Socialist Realism* (Berkeley, Calif.).

Firestone, Ross (ed.) (1972) *Getting Busted: Personal Experiences of Arrest, Trial and Prison* (Harmondsworth, Middx: Penguin Books).

Foulkes, A. P. (1975) *The Search for Literary Meaning: A Semiotic Approach to the Problem of Interpretation in Education* (Berne).

Franklin, Bruce (1972) 'The teaching of literature in the highest academies of the Empire', in Louis Kampf and Paul Lauter (eds), *The Politics of Literature* (New York), 101–29.

Fromm, Erich (1951) *The Forgotten Language* (New York).

Frye, Northrop (1964) *The Educated Imagination* (Bloomington, Ind. and London).

Gardner, Brian (ed.) (1964) *Up the Line to Death: The War Poets 1914–1918* (London).

Gibian, George and Tjalsma, H. W. (eds) (1976) *Russian Modernism – Culture and the Avant-Garde, 1900–1930* (Ithaca, NY).

Griffith, Robert (1970) *The Politics of Fear: Joseph McCarthy and the Senate* (Lexington, Ky).

Haase, Horst, Geerdts, Hans Jürgen, Kühne, Erich and Paulus, Walter (eds) (1976) *Geschichte der Literatur der Deutschen Demokratischen Republik* (Berlin).

Hahn, Ulla (1978) *Literatur in der Aktion: Zur Entwicklung operativer Literaturformen in der Bundesrepublik* (Wiesbaden).

Harari, Josué V. (ed.) (1980) *Textual Strategies: Perspectives in Post-Structuralist Criticism* (London).

Haste, Cate (1977) *Keep the Home Fires Burning: Propaganda in the First World War* (London).

Hawkes, Terence (1977) *Structuralism and Semiotics* (London).

Hecht, Werner (ed.) (1964) *Materialien zu Brechts 'Mutter Courage und ihre Kinder'* (Frankfurt).

Hofstadter, Richard (1966) *The Paranoid Style in American Politics and Other Essays* (London).

James, C. Vaughan (1973) *Soviet Socialist Realism: Origins and Theory* (New York).

Jameson, Fredric (1981) *The Political Unconscious: Narrative as a Socially Symbolic Act* (London).

Janouch, Gustav (1961) *Gespräche mit Kafka* (Frankfurt).

Juhl, P. D. (1980) *Interpretation: An Essay in the Philosophy of Literary Criticism* (Princeton, NJ).

Kafka, Franz (1961) *The Penal Colony, Stories and Short Pieces*, trans. by Willa and Edwin Muir (New York).

Kampf, Louis and Lauter, Paul (eds) (1972) *The Politics of Literature: Dissenting Essays on the Teaching of English* (New York).

Klemperer, Victor (1969) *LTI – Die unbewältigte Sprache* (Munich).

Kracauer, Siegfried (1957) 'National types as Hollywood presents them', in Bernard Rosenberg and David Manning White (eds), *Mass Culture, The Popular Arts in America* (New York), 257–77.

Kramnick, Isaac (1980) 'Children's literature and bourgeois ideology: observations on culture and industrial capitalism in the later eighteenth century', in Perez Zagorin (ed.), *Culture and Politics From Puritanism to the Enlightenment* (Berkeley, Calif.), 203–40.

Kuhns, Richard (1972) 'Semantics for Literary Languages', *New Literary History*, 4, 91–105.

Kuznetsov, Felix (1980) *Of Human Values: Soviet Literature Today* (Moscow).

Labedz, Leopold and Hayward, Max (eds) (1967) *On Trial, The Case of Sinyavsky (Tertz) and Daniel (Arzhak)* (London).

Lasswell, Harold D., Leites, Nathan and Associates (1965) *Language of Politics: Studies in Quantitative Semantics* (Cambridge, Mass.: MIT Press).

Levin, Harry (1973) ' "A matter of national concern": the report of the Commission on Obscenity and Pornography', in Joseph P. Strelka (ed.), *Yearbook of Comparative Criticism* (University Park, Pa.: Pennsylvania SU Press), 107–23.

Lyons, John (1968) *Introduction to Theoretical Linguistics* (Cambridge, England).

Marcuse, Herbert (1964) *One-Dimensional Man: Studies in the Ideology of Advanced Industrial Society* (London).

Miller, Arthur (1957) *Collected Plays* (New York).

Moltmann, Günter (1964) 'Goebbels' Rede zum totalen Krieg am 18. Februar 1943', *Vierteljahreshefte für Zeitgeschichte*, I, 13–43.

Morris, Charles (1971) *Writings on the General Theory of Signs* (The Hague).

Mueller, Claus (1973) *The Politics of Communication* (New York).

Neale, Steve (1977) 'Propaganda', *Screen*, 3, 9–40.

Orwell, George (1970) *The Collected Essays, Journalism and Letters*, vol. 2, Sonia Orwell and Ian Angus (eds) (Harmondsworth, Middx: Penguin Books).

Orwell, George (1980) *Animal Farm and Other Novels* (London).

Pearson, Carol (1981) 'Beyond government: anarchist feminism in the utopian novels of Dorothy Bryant, Marge Piercy and Mary Staton', *Alternative Futures: The Journal of Utopian Studies*, 126–35.

Plato (1951 edn) *The Republic of Plato*, trans. by F. M. Cornford (Oxford).

Potter, Beatrix (n.d.) *The Tale of Squirrel Nutkin* (London).

Quine, Willard V. (1964) 'Meaning and translation', in Jerry A. Fodor and Jerrold J. Katz (eds), *The Structure of Language: Readings in the Philosophy of Language* (Englewood Cliffs, NJ), 460–78.

Raskin, Jonah (1967) 'Imperialism: Conrad's Heart of Darkness', in Walter Laqueur and George L. Mosse (eds), *Literature and Politics in the Twentieth Century – Journal of Contemporary History*, vol. 5, 109–27.

Rich, Adrienne (1977) *Of Woman Born: Motherhood as Experience and Institution* (New York).

Rischbieter, Henning (1967) *Peter Weiss* (Hannover).

Rockwell, Joan (1974) *Fact in Fiction* (London).

Rovere, Richard H. (1962) *The American Establishment and Other Reports, Opinions and Speculations* (New York).

Rühle, Jürgen (1969) *Literature and Revolution: A Critical Study of the Writer and Communism in the Twentieth Century*, trans. and ed. by Jean Steinberg (London).

Sammons, Jeffrey L. (1977) *Literary Sociology and Practical Criticism* (Bloomington, Ind.).

Scholes, Robert (1974) *Structuralism in Literature* (New Haven, Conn.).

Shklovsky, Victor (1965) 'Art as technique', in *Russian Formalist Criticism*, trans. and ed. by Lee T. Lemon and Marion J. Reis (Lincoln, Nebr.).

Slotkin, Richard (1973) *Regeneration Through Violence: The Mythology of The American Frontier* (Middletown, Conn.: Wesleyan University Press).

Solomon, Maynard (ed.) (1979) *Marxism and Art* (Brighton, Sussex; first publ. 1972, New York).

Strothmann, Dietrich (1963) *Nationalsozialistische Literaturpolitik: Ein Beitrag zur Publizistik im Dritten Reich* (Bonn).

Szanto, George H. (1978) *Theater and Propaganda* (Austin, Tex.).

Taylor, Richard (1979) *Film Propaganda: Nazi Germany and Soviet Russia* (London).

Taylor, Ronald (1980) *Literature and Society in Germany 1918–1945* (Brighton, Sussex: Harvester Press and New York: Barnes & Noble).

Tomashevsky, Boris (1965) 'Thematics', in *Russian Formalist Criticism*, trans. and ed. by Lee T. Lemon and Marion J. Reis (Lincoln, Nebr.).

Wagenbach, Klaus, Stephan, Winfried and Krüger, Michael (eds) (1979) *Vaterland, Muttersprache – Deutsche Schriftsteller und ihr Staat seit 1945* (Berlin).

Wallraff, Günter (1973) 'Wirkungen in der Praxis', in Beate Pinkerneil, Dietrich Pinkerneil and Victor Žmegač (eds), *Literatur und Gesellschaft: Zur Sozialgeschichte der Literatur seit der Jahrhundertwende, eine Dokumentation* (Frankfurt), 263–8.

Wallraff, Günter (1976) *Die Reportagen* (Cologne).

Wallraff, Günter (1977) *Der Aufmacher: Der Mann der bei 'Bild' Hans Esser war* (Cologne).

Wallraff, Günter (1979) *Zeugen der Anklage: Die 'Bild'-beschreibung wird fortgesetzt* (Cologne).

Wallraff, Günter (1981) *Das 'Bild'-Handbuch* (Hamburg).

Warshow, Robert (1953) 'The liberal conscience in *The Crucible:* Arthur Miller and his audience', *Commentary* (March) 265–71.

Weales, Gerald (ed.) (1977) *Arthur Miller 'The Crucible'*, *Text and Criticism* (Harmondsworth, Middx: Penguin Books).

Weimann, Robert (1974) *'New Criticism' und die Entwicklung bürgerlicher Literaturwissenschaft* (Munich).

Wellek, René (1976) 'Russian Formalism', in George Gibian and H. W. Tjalsma (eds), *Russian Modernism – Culture and the Avant-Garde, 1900–1930* (Ithaca, NY), 31–48.

Wellek, René and Warren, Austin (1956) *Theory of Literature* (New York).

Whorf, B.·L. (1956) *Language, Thought and Reality. Selected Writings*, in John B. Carroll (ed.) (Cambridge, Mass.: MIT Press).

Willett, John (ed. and trans.) (1964) *Brecht on Theatre* (New York).

Williams, Emlyn (1981) *The Corn is Green* (London; first performed 1938).

Zagorin, Perez (ed.) (1980) *Culture and Politics From Puritanism to the Enlightenment* (Berkeley, Calif.).

Zamyatin, Yevgeny (1924) *We*, trans. by Gregory Zilboorg (New York).

Zhdanov, Andrei A. (1950) *Literature, Philosophy and Music* (New York).

Zima, Peter V. (1980) *Textsoziologie: Eine kritische Einführung* (Stuttgart).

Index